HELP!

A Practical Guide to Life's Ups and Downs

London: HMSO

Researched and written by Publishing Services, Central Office of Information.

© Crown copyright 1996
Applications for reproduction should be made to HMSO Copyright Unit, St Crispins, Duke Street, Norwich NR3 1PD
First published 1996

ISBN 0 11 701858 9

Published by HMSO and available from:

HMSO Publications Centre
(Mail, fax and telephone orders only)
PO Box 276, London, SW8 5DT
Telephone orders 0171-873 9090
General enquiries 0171-873 0011
(queuing system in operation for both numbers)
Fax orders 0171-873 8200

HMSO Bookshops
49 High Holborn, London, WC1V 6HB
(counter service only)
0171-873 0011 Fax 0171-831 1326
68–69 Bull Street, Birmingham B4 6AD
0121-236 9696 Fax 0121-236 9699
33 Wine Street, Bristol, BS1 2BQ
0117 9264306 Fax 0117 9294515
9-21 Princess Street, Manchester, M60 8AS
0161-834 7201 Fax 0161-833 0634
16 Arthur Street, Belfast, BT1 4GD
01232 238451 Fax 01232 235401
71 Lothian Road, Edinburgh, EH3 9AZ
0131-228 4181 Fax 0131-229 2734
The HMSO Oriel Bookshop
The Friary, Cardiff CF1 4AA
01222 395548 Fax 01222 384347

HMSO's Accredited Agents
(see Yellow Pages)

and through good booksellers

Contents

Preface

Are you a householder? A parent? A taxpayer? A pensioner? Do you ever use public transport or visit your GP? Ever need the help of a lawyer, a builder or the social services? And do you ever wonder about your legal rights when you want to complain about goods or services? If so, you will find this book an invaluable companion.

Help! contains a wealth of information on the rules and regulations that affect us all as husbands, wives or partners, citizens, consumers or travellers, workers, employers or users of health services. *Help!* looks at the main problems and procedures you may face in everyday life and tells you what action you should take, what choices you can make, your legal rights and the most effective way to complain.

For the householder *Help!* gives tips on buying and selling a property, renting and letting, saving energy in the home and what to do if you have difficulty paying bills.

As a family member, you can find out about how to register your baby's birth, 'do-it-yourself' divorce, your legal rights as an unmarried partner should the family home break up, and what to do when someone dies.

As a citizen, you can find out about serving on a jury, becoming a magistrate, voting at elections, even standing for Parliament. There's information, too, on your rights if you're arrested or if the police want to search your home.

Here's a book you can turn to for basic information on practically every aspect of daily living. So don't feel so anxious any more about what to do, how, when or where! *Help!* is at hand.

Introduction

All of us are affected by rules and procedures and often have to take important decisions as a result.

This book aims to identify the main dilemmas, problems and procedures that may confront you in your daily life. The guide covers your basic rights and responsibilities as citizen, householder, consumer, worker, employer, health services user and traveller.

Each section has been devised with the following questions in mind:

- what action should you take?
- what are you entitled to expect?
- what options exist for you? and
- what can you do if dissatisfied?

The text offers information and advice which is of initial help. It signposts the way to sources of further information and gives names and addresses where more detailed advice can be obtained.

The text is applicable to England and Wales. For rules and procedures relating to Scotland see *Your Rights and Responsibilities: A Personal Guide for Scottish Consumers*, published by the Scottish Consumer Council.

Although every attempt has been made to ensure that the book is accurate and up to date, it should not be regarded as offering a definitive view on legal matters.

The Central Office of Information (COI) would like to thank all those government departments and agencies and other organisations (in particular St John Ambulance, the Royal Society for the Prevention of Accidents and the National Association of Citizens Advice Bureaux) for their assistance in producing this publication.

HOME

Buying and selling a domestic property •

Renting and letting a dwelling •

Utilities •

Repairs, alterations, extensions • and planning

Safety in the home •

Energy conservation •

Buying and selling a domestic property

Fees and charges • Freehold or leasehold • Viewing properties •
Making an offer • Valuations and surveys • Conveyancing •
Exchanging contracts and completion • Setting a price •
Selling through an estate agent • Other selling options • Further information

- **FEES AND CHARGES** Fees and charges associated with buying and/or selling a property will include one or more of the following – legal fees, stamp duty, estate agents' fees, valuation and survey fees, search fees and furniture-removal expenses. If the property you propose to buy is leasehold there may be ground rents and service charges payable.

  If you need to borrow money for buying a property – that is, take out a mortgage – then contact several different lenders to find out how much they would be prepared to lend you. Alternatively, an independent financial adviser can advise you on the range of mortgages offered by different lenders. Most lending institutions base the amount they are prepared to advance you on multiples of a single or joint income. Check if there any properties they are not willing to lend on, for example, conversions or flats over commercial premises.

  Get some quotations from solicitors or conveyancers for handling the legal aspects of sale and purchase.

- **FREEHOLD OR LEASEHOLD** There are two main categories of domestic property on the market – **freehold** (where you purchase absolute ownership with no other parties involved) or **leasehold** (where the property returns to the owner when the lease expires). Leases generally run for 99 years; the value of a leasehold property may fall as it nears the lease expiry date. Leases often carry covenants which dictate the terms under which the property is leased to you. There may be an annual ground rent to pay to the freeholder, as well as service charges towards the repairs and upkeep of the property. These charges may be subject to regular increases. Under recent legislation you may be able to buy the freehold of the property.

- **VIEWING PROPERTIES** When you have decided on the type of property you want to buy and the location you prefer, look at the property pages of local newspapers and visit local estate agents to see what is available for sale.

Consider points which are important to you. Do you need to be close to public transport, shops or schools? Is there adequate parking if you own a car? View the property on several occasions and at different times of the day. Do not dismiss viewing a property that may be just above your price range as the owners may be open to offers on the selling price.

- **MAKING AN OFFER** Once you have found the right property make an offer either directly to the seller (vendor) or through the estate agent acting for them. The offer will be 'subject to contract'. You can make several offers at the same time on different properties, because an offer is not legally binding.

If your offer is accepted by the vendor and you are not carrying out your own conveyancing, you will need to engage a conveyancer or a solicitor and inform your chosen lending institution.

- **VALUATIONS AND SURVEYS** The lending institution will wish to satisfy itself that the property you have chosen offers sufficient security for the amount of money they are proposing to advance to you. They do this by carrying out a valuation, sometimes called a valuation survey and not to be confused with a structural survey. Although the buyer pays the fee for the valuation survey, he or she does not have the right to read the report. If the valuation of the property is found unacceptable, the buyer will still have to pay the fee.

In addition to the valuation survey, buyers may choose to have a structural survey carried out on the property by an independent surveyor. A structural survey is designed to give a reasonably accurate picture of the state of the property. The lender may offer a scheme where, for an extra fee, they will combine a valuation survey with a structural survey. A home energy rating (which will provide a measure of the level of energy efficiency of the property) may be available free as part of one of the above services.

- **CONVEYANCING** Conveyancing is the term for the legal formalities involved in buying or selling a home. It can be done by a solicitor or a conveyancer, or you can do it yourself (see Further information). The formalities include the local authority 'local land charges search' which should reveal details about the planning history of the property and any future or planned developments which may affect the value.

- **EXCHANGING CONTRACTS AND COMPLETION** Once all the legal formalities have been completed and the lending institution has made a formal 'offer of advance' which is acceptable to you, contracts between you and the vendor can be exchanged. Both the buyer and the vendor can change their minds up to the time of exchange, but remain liable for the fees they have incurred up to that point.

At exchange of contracts you may be asked to put down a deposit, usually 5 or 10 per cent. A completion date will be agreed, usually around four weeks hence. On the day of completion the solicitors or conveyancers acting for the buyer and the vendor arrange for the balance of the money due on the property to be transferred. The title deeds of the property transferring 'title' (ownership) are then released. The property has now changed ownership. In most cases the lending institution will keep the title deeds until the mortgage has been repaid.

- **SELLING A PROPERTY: SETTING A PRICE** Most sellers rely on estate agents to put a value on the property. If you approach an estate agent for a valuation, make it clear that you are not necessarily asking them to handle the sale. It is advisable to obtain several valuations from different agents. Many do not charge for this service. Be realistic about any shortcomings the property may have when finalising the selling price. For instance, the property may not have central heating or a garage. Similarly, if the property has special features these should be taken into account. Be prepared for buyers to negotiate.

- **SELLING THROUGH AN ESTATE AGENT** Estate agents' fees can range from 1–3 per cent plus VAT on the final selling price, depending on the terms of engagement. For example, sole agency – where only one agent is instructed to sell – may incur a lower fee than a multi-agency arrangement, where several agents are instructed to sell and whichever succeeds gets the commission. Contact several estate agents for quotations.

It may be possible to negotiate a reduced fee. Confirm in writing the basis on which you have engaged an agency. Be sure that you only agree to pay commission if the sale goes through. If you grant an estate agent sole agency rights it is advisable to place a time limit on them to effect a sale (usually six to eight weeks).

Estate agents may not make false or misleading statements. If you have a complaint to make about an agent contact your local authority trading standards (or consumer protection) department.

• **OTHER SELLING OPTIONS** You may decide to sell your property yourself, in which case you will need to set your own price and pay for any advertising you require. You will need to have the time to deal with enquiries and show the property to prospective buyers. If you accept an offer you will need to inform your solicitor or conveyancer of the full details of the sale.

Alternatively, you may decide to sell your property by auction rather than by private treaty. Purchase by auction is binding, but remember that the property may not reach the 'reserve' or minimum price that you are prepared to accept.

FURTHER INFORMATION

For more details about the system of transfer of property in England and Wales you can consult the relevant chapters in the following publications:

• Buying, selling and moving home by David Lewis (a teach yourself book published by Hodder and Stoughton).
• The Daily Mail – Buying and selling a house or flat by Howard and Jackie Green (published by Kogan Page).
• The streetwise guide to buying & selling your home by Martin Village (published by Judy Piatkus Ltd).

For do-it-yourself conveyancing consult:
• DIY conveyancing – a practical guide to the legal aspects of buying and selling a house by Robert T. Steele (published by David & Charles Publishers).

Addresses
• **National Association of Estate Agents,** Arbon House, 21 Jury Street, Warwick CV34 4EH (Tel. 01926 496800).
• **Incorporated Society of Valuers and Auctioneers (ISVA),** 3 Cadogan Gate, London SWIX 0AS (Tel. 0171 235 2282).
• **Royal Institution of Charted Surveyors,** 12 Great George Street, London SWIP 3AD (Tel. 0171 222 7000).
• **Ombudsman for Corporate Estate Agents,** Beckett House, 4 Bridge Street, Salisbury, Wiltshire SP1 2LX (Tel. 01722 333306).
• **Building Societies Association,** 3 Savile Row, London WIX IAF (Tel. 0171 437 0655).

Renting and letting a dwelling

Legislation • Regulated tenancy • Assured tenancy •
Assured shorthold tenancy • Licences and non-assured lettings •
Public sector tenants • Repairs • Possession proceedings • Harassment •
Further information

Landlords and tenants have certain basic responsibilities and obligations. Tenants should pay any rent on time, take reasonable care of the property or any of the landlord's furniture or other belongings, and give the landlord reasonable access to effect any repairs. Landlords should keep the property in a habitable condition and the structure and exterior properly maintained.

It is important for tenants and landlords to understand what type of tenancy they have, are being offered, or are offering. If you are in any doubt about your legal rights or obligations ask for information from a Citizens Advice Bureau or see a solicitor. The whole area of housing law is extremely complex, and so the information below can provide only a very general outline.

• **LEGISLATION** Private sector lettings (from an individual, a housing association or company) which began on or after 15 January 1989 are, for the most part, regulated by the Housing Act 1988 in England and Wales. Most private tenants who began renting before January 1989 continue to be protected by the Rent Act 1977.

The Housing Act 1985 applies to lettings by providers of public housing, such as local authorities, housing trusts, urban development corporations and housing associations (although new lettings by housing associations after 15 January 1989 were placed within the same framework as private sector tenants).

- **REGULATED TENANCY** If a tenancy is within the protection of the 1977 Rent Act, it is known as a regulated tenancy. This means that the tenant or landlord has the right to apply to the local rent officer (see under Rent Officer Service in your phone book) for the registration of a fair rent, and that the tenant has security of tenure (that is, the tenant cannot be evicted except by court order in certain specified circumstances). An appeal against a rent officer's decision can be made to the rent assessment committee. Since the 1988 Housing Act came into force in January 1989, it has not generally been possible to create a new regulated tenancy, although the above protection remains for existing regulated tenancies.

- **ASSURED TENANCY** From January 1989 new private sector lettings were deregulated, and two new forms of tenancy were introduced – the assured tenancy and the assured shorthold tenancy. The duration and terms of an assured tenancy, including rent and rent review, are negotiated between the parties involved. The tenant is advised to ask for a written statement of the terms and will have security of tenure except in certain circumstances. The tenant does not have the right to ask a rent officer or rent assessment committee to set a market rent, except when a rent review is due and landlord and tenant fail to agree.

- **ASSURED SHORTHOLD TENANCY** This type of tenancy is for a fixed term of at least six months, and the rent is a matter for negotiation between the parties. The landlord must serve a notice on the tenant before the start of the lease informing him or her that it is a shorthold let, because at the end of the fixed term the landlord has a mandatory ground for possession, subject to two months' notice.

- **LICENCES AND NON-ASSURED LETTINGS** Lettings are generally regarded as tenancies if the accommodation is self-contained and the landlord is not resident. Lettings which are not tenancies may be licences to occupy. Licensees have fewer rights than tenants. In cases of doubt, legal advice should be sought.

Some tenancies created on or after 15 January 1989 will not be assured tenancies. These include lettings by certain educational institutions to students; holiday lets; those where there is a resident landlord; and those where, for a period of less than 12 months, a local authority enters into an arrangement with a private landlord for temporary accommodation for applicants with a priority need, such as the homeless.

- **PUBLIC SECTOR TENANTS** Legislation in 1985 gives security of tenure to many tenants of local authorities and certain other bodies. Subject to certain conditions, such tenants also have the right to buy their homes at a discount price.

Under the Tenant's Choice provisions, council tenants have the right to change their landlord. The aim of this is to increase choice for tenants, expose local authority housing to competition, and raise service standards. Properly constituted tenants' associations also have the right to set up management organisations and take over the running of their estates.

- **REPAIRS** Obligations on the landlord to carry out repairs are implied by the Landlord and Tenant Act 1985 and cover most weekly or monthly lets and fixed terms of less than seven years. They apply to most private tenancies and to lettings by local authorities. Under the obligations a landlord must keep in reasonable repair:

- the structure and exterior of the premises;

- the installations for gas, water and electricity; and

- those for space heating and heating water.

In the case of blocks of flats, where tenancies have been granted for less than seven years on or after 15 January 1989, the landlord may also be responsible for the repairs of most common parts of the building and installations (such as central heating boilers) if they are owned by or under the landlord's control.

- **POSSESSION PROCEEDINGS** A landlord can usually bring an assured tenancy to an end only by serving notice on the tenant of his or her intention to seek possession. The notice must state the grounds on which possession will be sought and the period of the notice depends on these grounds. If the tenant does not leave, the landlord must apply in the county court for an order for possession. Tenants who are protected by the Rent Act 1977, the Housing Act 1985 or the Housing Act 1988 cannot be evicted other than by a court order.

- **HARASSMENT** It is a criminal offence for a landlord or anyone else unlawfully to evict or harass a tenant. Harassment can take the form of threats or physical violence, or persistent disconnections of gas, electricity or water supplies. A tenant who is being harassed should report it to the police.

FURTHER INFORMATION

- The **Department of the Environment**, in conjunction with the **Welsh Office**, has published a series of booklets on housing matters. They are free and you can get copies from rent officers, Citizens Advice Bureaux, housing aid centres and local authorities.

- The charity **Shelter** also publishes helpful booklets and guides for tenants. You can contact **Shelter** at 88 Old Street, London EC1V 9HU (Tel. 0171 253 0202).

Utilities

Electricity • Gas • Water • Telephone • Further information

• **ELECTRICITY** Domestic consumers receive electricity from public electricity suppliers; these comprise 12 regional companies in England and Wales. The Office of Electricity Regulation (OFFER) is an independent body set up in 1989 to regulate the electricity supply industry.

Are there any standards of service which the electricity company must maintain?

Each electricity company must maintain set customer-service performance standards. Ten Guaranteed Standards set service levels which, if not met, result in a fixed payment to the customer. These include the keeping of appointments, the restoration of electricity supplies within 24 hours, and prompt response to estimates and complaints. Your electricity company (listed in the phone book under Electricity) will provide full details of guaranteed services, or you can contact OFFER at the address on p. 21.

Eight overall standards govern other customer services, for which targets are set. Each electricity company also has to work within codes of practice approved by OFFER.

What can I do if I have a problem paying my bill?

If you have a problem paying your bill it is important that you contact your electricity company. If you are in genuine difficulty, the electricity company must offer easy payment arrangements to collect the debt. An alternative method of payment, such as a prepayment meter, may be offered. Your electricity supply may be cut off if you do not pay your bill or keep to the payment arrangements. If all the people in the house are of pensionable age, the electricity supply will not be cut off between 1 October and 31 March if the bill cannot be paid.

What should I do when I move house?

You need to give two working days' notice for both the connection and disconnection of your electricity supply. For the connection of electricity you may need to provide proof of identity and your previous address. If you cannot provide this proof you may be asked to provide some form of security – for example, a security deposit – or enter into a direct debit arrangement. You may also be asked for a security if you are not considered creditworthy, if you rent your home or if you have been a late payer and do not agree to a prepayment method.

How do I complain?

If you have a complaint, you should first contact your local electricity company. If you are not satisfied with the response of the company, contact OFFER. Your local office is usually listed on the back of your electricity bill. An independent Electricity Consumers' Committee may also consider some complaints.

If your complaint does not relate to the electricity company's supply activities (that is, if it is a complaint about retail or contracting activities), you may need to approach your local Citizens Advice Bureau for advice.

- **GAS** The Gas Act 1986 established the regulatory regime for the private gas sector and places responsibility on the independent Office of Gas Supply (OFGAS) for the regulation of the gas industry. The Act also established the Gas Consumers Council, independent of both British Gas and OFGAS and responsible for investigating consumer complaints.

Must British Gas maintain set standards of service?

British Gas has established standards of service and, in some cases, if they are not met a payment is made as compensation to the customer. A gas supply which is disconnected for safety or maintenance/repair should be restored within 24 hours – otherwise, compensation is paid for each day or part of a day that you are without gas (except where the interruption is caused by circumstances beyond the company's control). Other payments are made for failure to keep appointments without proper notice. Your local Customer Service Centre will be able to provide details of standards of service. Look under Gas in your phone book for the address.

There is a legal requirement for firms who install gas appliances or work on any part of the gas system to be registered with the Council for Registered Gas Installers (CORGI – see p. 34).

If I think gas is escaping, will I have to pay call-out charges?

British Gas runs a 24-hour emergency service to deal with suspected gas escapes. There is a special number in the phone book under the Gas display advertisement to report gas escapes. The first 30 minutes of repair work, or all of the time needed to make the escape safe, will be free. This includes parts and materials up to a minimal value (£2.50 plus VAT). Parts and materials over this minimal value will be charged for, as will time taken for repair work over the specified 30 minutes.

What should I do when moving house?

British Gas requires at least 24 hours' notice before you move so that your bill can be calculated correctly. If the house you are moving to has an outside meter, you should have been left the key; if not, it will be replaced free of charge by British Gas. A quotation for the supply of gas must be provided within a specified time limit (five working days) unless a survey or visit is required.

What should I do if I have difficulty paying my gas bill?

If you have a problem paying your bill you should contact British Gas straight away. You may be offered a Gas Payment Plan arrangement or a prepayment meter (set at a level to contribute to arrears). A leaflet *How to get help if you can't pay your gas bill* is available from British Gas. Pensioners who cannot pay their gas bill will not have their supply cut off between 1 October and 31 March.

How do I make a complaint?

If you have a complaint contact British Gas first. If you do not get satisfaction, contact your local Gas Consumers Council. You can find the address in the phone book under Gas, or on the back of your gas bill. If your complaint relates to the supply of gas and cannot be settled, the Gas Consumers Council will involve OFGAS, which has powers to resolve disputes.

- **WATER** In England and Wales ten regional water and sewerage companies have statutory responsibilities for providing both water supply and sewage treatment. These regional companies provide all of the sewerage services and approximately three-quarters of water supply; the remaining 25 per cent is supplied by 21 water companies which provide water supply services only. To find the address of your local company look in the phone book under Water.

The Drinking Water Inspectorate has to ensure that drinking water is wholesome and that companies comply with the regulations. The Office of Water Services (OFWAT) is an independent government department responsible for ensuring that water and sewerage companies provide a good quality and efficient service at a fair price.

Are water companies regulated by a Code of Practice?
Under the terms of their operating licences water companies are required to publish Codes of Practice, including a Code on Disconnection Procedures. Water companies must also operate a Guaranteed Standards Scheme, with fixed compensation payments if certain standards are not met. Areas covered under the scheme include unplanned interruptions to water supply lasting longer than a specified period, the keeping of appointments and prompt response to queries or complaints. For some failures, compensation payments are automatically made within ten working days of the incident. Others may require the customer to make a claim in writing within three months of the incident. Compensation is not paid where exceptional circumstances (such as severe weather conditions) prevent the water company from meeting their standards.

What do I do if I cannot pay my bill?
If you have difficulty paying for your water supply contact the address shown on your water bill. Contact a Citizens Advice Bureau or consumer advice centre for independent advice. If you are in receipt of Income Support, the social security office may be able to arrange for direct payments to be made. If you do not pay your bill and do not contact the water company, your water may be cut off.

What should I do if I think there is something wrong with my drinking water?
Water companies have a legal obligation to supply wholesome water. If you think your water is not fit to drink you should contact the water company

immediately. They will try to be at your home within four hours of being informed. They will take a sample from your supply and send you a report. If you ask they will also send full details of their analysis.

How do I make a complaint?

If your complaint is about your bill for water or sewerage services, write to the address printed at the top of the bill. If your complaint is about any other part of the service, write to the Customer Service Department of your local water or sewerage company. All companies must have a procedure, approved by OFWAT, for dealing with customer complaints. You can ask your company for a free copy of its procedure.

If you have followed the company's complaints procedure but are still not satisfied, you can ask OFWAT's Customer Service Committee (CSC) to investigate. The address of your local CSC is in the phone book under OFWAT. Their service is free.

- **TELEPHONE** In 1984 British Telecom (BT) was reconstituted as a public limited company. The Office of Telecommunications (OFTEL) is the independent regulatory body for the telecommunications industry.

Does BT offer guaranteed standards of service?

BT's customer service guarantee scheme pays compensation if BT does not meet its guaranteed standards. Payment is at a fixed daily rate or, if the customer has lost money as a result of BT's error, actual financial loss may be compensated for. The standards include: meeting time limits to supply or repair a service; keeping appointments; ensuring that lines are not disconnected in error; and ensuring that customers do not suffer repeated loss of service. Claims for daily rate compensation can be made by calling freefone numbers 150 (residential customers) or 0800 800152 (business customers). Claims for actual financial loss must be made in writing, with supporting evidence – look on your phone bill for the address. Customers should claim any compensation within four months.

What should I do if I dispute the amount of my bill?

If you dispute your phone bill you should first complain to the Customer Service Manager; the address and freefone number will be on the back of the bill. If BT's complaint-handling procedure does not resolve your problem, you can take it up with BT's Complaints Review Service, which will investigate your complaint in detail. If you remain dissatisfied, you can refer the matter to OFTEL. Should you then wish to take the matter further, you can contact the Chartered Institute of Arbitrators. This offers an independent and free arbitration service, with the arbitrator making a decision based on the written evidence presented.

FURTHER INFORMATION

Addresses

- **Gas Consumers Council,** Abford House, 15 Wilton Road, London SW1V 1LT (Tel. 0171 931 9155).
- **Office of Electricity Regulation (OFFER),** Hagley House, 83–85 Hagley Road, Edgbaston, Birmingham B16 8QG (Tel. 0121 456 2100).
- **Office of Gas Supply (OFGAS),** Stockley House, 130 Wilton Road, London SW1V 1LQ (Tel. 0171 828 0898).
- **Office of Telecommunications (OFTEL),** 50 Ludgate Hill, London EC4M 7JJ (Tel. 0171 634 8700 Locall 0345 145000).
- **Office of Water Services (OFWAT),** Centre City Tower, 7 Hill Street, Birmingham B5 4UA (Tel. 0121 625 1300).

Repairs, alterations, extensions and planning

Before you start • Choosing a contractor • Contracts • Payment •
Legal rights • If things go wrong • Further information

• **BEFORE YOU START** If you are having repairs or alterations done to your home, plan what needs to be done in as much detail as possible. Professional advice from an architect or surveyor will almost certainly be necessary for large-scale projects. Depending on the nature of the work, you may need to get planning permission and/or building regulations consent from your local authority (see below). You will also need special clearance if you live in a conservation area or a listed building. Inform your neighbours about the work you are having done, particularly where party structures are involved.

Local authority approval

New building work, such as an extension or other structural project, will often need to comply with the building regulations, which are meant to ensure that the work conforms to specified health and safety standards. An application for planning permission is an application to be allowed to carry out development within the Town and Country Planning Acts. You should discuss the work you intend to have done with planning officers at your local authority planning department.

Converting a house or flat into two or more units or dividing part of your home for business or commercial use will nearly always require planning permission. Permission is also needed when alterations would affect the external appearance of the house. You should also ensure that there are no covenants or other restrictions in the title to your property, or conditions in the lease, stating that you need someone else's agreement to carry out work.

If the property is in a conservation area, or is 'listed' as being of historic or architectural interest, there will be many restrictions on any alteration. Trees can be the subject of preservation orders; if so, you will need local authority permission before you cut them down.

Applying for planning permission

Your local authority planning department will advise you how to apply. You can make an outline application to the authority if you want their response before making detailed drawings. Full applications should be sent with a plan of the site and a copy of the drawings showing the work you propose to carry out. The application should be decided within eight weeks.

What if permission is refused?

If permission is refused, or conditions imposed, the authority should give their reasons. You can submit another application with modified plans free of charge within 12 months of the decision on your first application. If you think the decision is unreasonable you can appeal to the Secretary of State for the Environment. Appeals have to be made within six months of the authority's decision.

If your planning problem is very complex, you can consider using a consultant Chartered Town Planner (listed in the *Directory of Planning Consultants*) for independent advice, although fees for this service can be expensive.

● **CHOOSING A CONTRACTOR** If you do not know any reliable contractors, ask friends and neighbours or relevant trade associations whether they can recommend anyone. If you are using a surveyor or architect, they may be able to help. Look for an established trader and ask to see work similar to your requirements that the contractor has carried out. Find out whether the firm belongs to a trade association, as it may have a protection scheme or be able to help resolve disputes.

Do not agree to have work done just because someone knocks on your door and tells you that, for example, your roof needs repairing. If you are interested, check the company out first and give yourself time to get estimates from other traders for comparison. Beware of trade cards which come through the door, particularly if there is only a phone number.

Invite three or four traders to cost the job. Give them a detailed job specification and state clearly that you want a firm price. This is usually known as a quotation, whereas an estimate is a rough price. A firm price is binding, whatever it is called. Compare the quotations, bearing in mind that the cheapest may not necessarily be the best.

- **GETTING A CONTRACT** Get a written agreement or contract covering all the important points: the work to be done, the price, how long the job will take, how and when payment will be made. Read it carefully.

Make sure there is a completion date if it is important that the work is finished by a particular time, with details of compensation for any delay.

For larger jobs, **a standard industry contract** is probably appropriate, such as the JCT Minor Works contract. This covers all the main points and is available from the Royal Institute of British Architects (see p. 26 for address).

- **MAKING PAYMENTS** Stage payments are a good way of ensuring the steady progress of the work, as you are paying for work that has been satisfactorily completed. If not, you have a means to apply pressure to the contractor. Agree how and when payments will be made in the contract.

In general, you should not pay in advance. There is a risk that the contractor might disappear with the money. There is also less incentive to proceed with the job. If you are asked for money to pay for specialist materials, it is better to order the goods yourself and have them delivered direct to you. Small businesses may ask for deposits for materials which they do not keep in stock. Think carefully whether this is necessary and whether the amount is fair. Do not pay a lump sum to cover materials for the whole job, only pay for those which are needed at any particular stage.

Include in your contract that you will retain a sum (10 per cent might be appropriate) for an agreed period after the work is completed. This allows you time to check that the job has been properly carried out, and is the best way to ensure that the trader will put right any faults.

- **WHAT ARE MY LEGAL RIGHTS?** Under the Supply of Goods and Services Act 1982, a service must be carried out:

- with reasonable care and skill;

- within a reasonable time; and

- at a reasonable charge if no price has been fixed at the outset.

(See under **Consumer rights** – p. 142).

Any materials supplied as part of a service must be as described by the contractor, of satisfactory quality and fit for the purpose for which they are intended. If you insist on using certain materials, you will not be able to claim from the contractor if they turn out to be unsuitable.

- **WHAT IF THINGS GO WRONG?** Start by discussing the problem, giving the contractor the chance to put things right. If you are not satisfied, put your complaint in writing, saying what you want done and setting a deadline. Keep copies of letters, a note of phone calls and a diary of events if appropriate. It may be worth getting an expert opinion to back up your complaint. This may cost money but could be invaluable if you have to take legal action.

Consider withholding any further payment until the matter is resolved – check your contract first. Be careful if you are paying by credit as there may be problems if you fall behind with your payments. It is probably advisable to get expert guidance on this.

If the contractor is a member of a trade association, there may be a conciliation or arbitration scheme you can use. You also have the option of taking the contractor to court using the small claims procedure (see p. 145). You can get guidance from your local Citizens Advice Bureau, trading standards department or consumer advice centre.

FURTHER INFORMATION

The booklets Planning – a guide for householders *and* Building regulations – a guide for owners of small businesses and for householders *are available from your local council or from the* **Department of the Environment,** *P.O. Box 135, Bradford, West Yorkshire BD9 4HU.*

Addresses

- **British Wood Preserving and Damp-proofing Association,** Building No. 6, The Office Village, 4 Romford Road, London E15 4EA (Tel. 0181 519 2588).
- **Electrical Contractors' Association,** 34 Palace Court, London W2 4HY (Tel. 0171 229 1266).
- **Federation of Master Builders,** 14–15 Great James Street, London WC1N 3DP (Tel. 0171 242 7583/7).

- **Glass and Glazing Federation,** 44–48 Borough High Street, London SE1 1XB (Tel. 0171 403 7177).
- **Heating and Ventilating Contractors' Association,** 34 Palace Court, London W2 4JG (Tel. 0171 229 2488).
- **National Inspection Council for Electrical Installation Contracting,** Vintage House, 37 Albert Embankment, London SE1 7UJ (Tel. 0171 582 7746).
- **Royal Institute of British Architects,** Clients' Advisory Service, 66 Portland Place, London W1N 4AD (Tel. 0171 580 5533).
- **Royal Institution of Chartered Surveyors,** Information Centre, Surveyor Court, Westwood Way, Coventry CV4 8JE (Tel. 01203 694757).

Safety in the home

Where and when accidents occur • Home safety assessment •
Safety practices and standards • Further information

Accidents in the home account for just over one-third of all accidental injuries in Britain each year – around 3.4 million – outstripping those in the workplace or on the roads. Human error is one of the main factors in a high percentage of home accidents. Most at risk are the under-five age group and the over-65s, but everybody can benefit by identifying and taking steps to minimise hazards.

- **WHERE AND WHEN ACCIDENTS OCCUR** Most accidents occur in the living or dining room, followed by the kitchen, garden, stairway and lastly the bedroom. Falls are the most common accidents; many result in fractures, particularly among older people. Burns and scalds are high on the list in all age groups, with choking and poisoning most common among the under-fives. Instances of choking are mostly due to children swallowing small objects. Cases of poisoning usually result from household chemicals and medicines not being safely stored (although such risks are being reduced with the introduction of child-resistant closures on many medicine containers).

A large majority of non-fatal injuries in the home, including those from do-it-yourself activities and gardening, involve cuts, bruises, lacerations and swellings. The most common fatal injuries are from serious falls, poisoning (including that from carbon monoxide fumes due to faulty heating equipment), choking, and from outbreaks of fire (including those originating from household appliances).

Many accidents occur at times of stress, very often when a routine is changed, or when someone is in a hurry or distracted. Inadequate supervision of small children and pets also poses a danger.

• **HOME SAFETY ASSESSMENT** You can help to reduce the danger of accidents by evaluating each area of your home for potential hazards. For example, is there sufficient natural or artificial light where there are steps or stairs? Are walkways clear of obstructions? Are fixtures and fittings properly secure and in working order? Are movable or dangerous items out of the reach of small children?

To help you identify potential trouble spots, you can get copies of the free guides *Stay Safe At Home,* published by the Department of Trade and Industry's Consumer Safety Unit, and *Making Your Home Safe,* produced by Boots the Chemists in conjunction with the Child Accident Prevention Trust. You can also ask your local authority whether they have a home safety officer who can give appropriate advice.

• **SAFETY PRACTICES AND STANDARDS** A priority in any home is an adequately stocked first-aid pack. For advice on what to carry, you can ask your local health visitor or health education unit. Have a leaflet handy outlining the 'ABC of resuscitation' procedure or preferably attend a first-aid training course (for which contact St John Ambulance or the British Red Cross – see p. 93).

If you are a new parent, ask your local family clinic for advice about safety measures for infants.

To minimise the threat from fire, it is essential to have a smoke alarm installed. The use of fire extinguishers in the home is not recommended, since the first priority when fire breaks out is to get yourself and anybody else out of the property. People die trying to fight fires because they do not understand how little time they have before fumes become lethal. It is acceptable, however, to have a fire blanket readily to hand to deal quickly with situations like chip pan fires. You can get guidance on fire prevention measures from your local fire brigade.

Make sure that, where possible, items bought for the home are kitemarked by a British Standard number (see p. 148), and follow the manufacturer's handling and operating instructions carefully. Have electrical and gas appliances and fittings checked and serviced regularly by qualified technicians.

FURTHER INFORMATION

Further practical advice and guidance, including leaflets and factsheets, on home safety can be obtained from the:

- **Royal Society for the Prevention of Accidents (RoSPA),** The Priory Queensway, Birmingham B4 6BS (Tel. 0121 200 2461).

- **Child Accident Prevention Trust (CAPT),** 4th floor, Clerk's Court, 18–20 Farringdon Lane, London EC1R 3AU (Tel. 0171 608 3828).

- **Department of Trade and Industry (Consumer Safety Unit),** 10–18 Victoria Street, London SW1H 0NN (Tel. 0171 215 3215).

Energy conservation

Insulation • Heating • Domestic appliances • Motoring • Further information

- **ENERGY CONSERVATION** Conserving energy has both financial and environmental benefits. The more energy efficient you make your home, the lower your fuel bills will be; your home can also be warmer and more comfortable. Burning fossil fuels releases carbon dioxide (CO_2) into the atmosphere, and over a quarter of the CO_2 produced in Britain comes from energy used in the home. The United Nations Convention on Climate Change, signed by Britain in 1992, commits developed countries to reduce significantly emissions of CO_2 and other greenhouse gases.

What are the most effective ways to conserve energy in the home?
Energy is conserved most effectively by proper insulation to retain heat and by using energy-efficient heating systems and appliances. The Department of the Environment has issued two helpful leaflets *Insulating Your Home* and *Heating Your Home*. You can also ask at your local gas and electricity customer service centres for advice.

In addition local energy advice centres offer free, impartial and independent advice on energy-saving measures in homes, designed to help reduce fuel bills. To find out if there is a centre near you, ring the Energy Saving Trust on 0171 931 8401.

Where should I insulate my home to retain heat?
Heat escapes from your house through cracks and gaps between doors, floors and windows, which also allow cold air to enter. Blocking off the

gaps can be fairly inexpensive, using draught excluders and seals. However, you should maintain ventilation in those rooms where gas, oil or solid fuel appliances are used, since these need fresh air to work properly and safely. Kitchens and bathrooms also need ventilation to avoid condensation. Lofts should always be insulated, and cavity wall insulation will retain a large amount of heat. Covering your hot water tank with an insulating jacket will soon pay for itself in lower fuel bills. You should also insulate hot water pipes to stop heat escaping from them.

What about double glazing?
Double glazing can halve the amount of heat lost through windows. Though expensive, it is especially worth considering for windows that face north and have large amounts of glass. If you intend to have double glazing fitted, you should ask for quotes from three or four different contractors before you decide. If you have double or secondary glazing, always be sure that you can escape in an emergency, such as a fire. Cheap do-it-yourself alternatives to double glazing include thin, flexible plastic sheets or fixed panels.

Insulating lofts and floors
Loft insulation should be 200mm (8in) deep to be effective. Use mineral fibre mat or roll; never use flammable material. Do not insulate beneath water tanks situated on or just above the floor of the loft. Insulating materials can irritate the throat or skin, so you should protect yourself with a mask, gloves and goggles during installation.

Wall-to-wall carpets help to stop heat going through the floor, and should have a good rubber or felt underlay. Gaps between floorboards and under skirting boards can be filled up with newspaper, beading, mastic or plastic wood.

Wall insulation
Cavity wall insulation must be installed by a professional contractor, but will usually take less than a day to do. Solid walls can be insulated internally by an experienced handyman, but external solid wall insulation is more expensive and must be carried out by a specialist contractor.

If you are installing a conservatory you should retain the wall and any existing doors between the living space and the conservatory. Build on to a south wall preferably, or east or west facing walls.

Are there other ways to reduce heat loss?
Using lined or insulated curtains will help to keep heat in. Make sure that they do not drape over radiators or hang in front of them, as heat will then be funnelled out of the window. If you have radiators fitted against an outside wall, use aluminium foil behind them to prevent the heat going through the wall. Fixing a shelf above a radiator will deflect warm air towards the middle of the room rather than letting it rise to the ceiling. Blocking off unused chimneys can help reduce heat loss but there should be air grilles in them to avoid condensation and provide ventilation.

Is there help available for low-income families to insulate their home?
The Home Energy Efficiency Scheme (HEES) may be able to provide a grant for low-income families, people who are disabled and those aged over 60 towards the cost of draught-proofing and loft, tank and pipe insulation. HEES is administered by the Energy Action Grants Agency (EAGA) on behalf of the Department of the Environment.

Can I use my heating system more efficiently?
Central heating systems should be fitted with thermostats and timers, allowing you to control the temperature level and the times at which the heating comes on and goes off. Fitting thermostatic radiator valves (TRVs) lets you control the temperature of each room separately. Modern boilers are normally more efficient than older models and condensing boilers are the most efficient. Only have the heating on when it is needed. Constant background heating is only necessary when the temperature is freezing, or to protect your pipes from freezing when you go away.

If you do not have central heating make sure that individual heaters are the right size for the room. Electric storage heaters store heat at night when electricity is available at a lower rate. Gas and electricity showrooms will give advice on energy-efficient systems. Heating systems should be serviced annually.

Heating water can account for as much as 20 per cent of the average fuel bill. Taking a shower uses only two-fifths the amount of water as a bath.

How can I use domestic appliances more efficiently?

The more you cook at any one time, the more energy you save. Use pans, with lids, that are the right size for what you are cooking and for the size of your cooker. Overfilling kettles wastes energy, though you do need to cover the element. Regular use of a descaler will make the kettle more efficient. A toaster uses less energy than the grill.

If you need to buy a new fridge, or other appliance, look for one with the European Community energy efficiency label or compare energy usage information in manufacturers' brochures. Defrost fridge/freezers regularly. Keep freezers at least three-quarters full and check that the door seal fits properly. The fridge door should be open as briefly as possible. Position the fridge away from any source of heat such as a boiler and keep the radiator panel at the back well ventilated.

Wait until you have a full load before using your washing machine, otherwise use an economy programme. Do not leave lights on unnecessarily and use dimmer switches where convenient. Fluorescent energy-saving bulbs can last ten times as long as an ordinary bulb but use around a quarter of the electricity. However they are more expensive.

Can I make my driving more energy efficient?

When you choose a car, take into account its fuel economy and choose one with a catalytic converter, which cleans up the exhaust emissions. Use unleaded petrol if possible. Driving at high speeds uses more fuel than at low speeds. You should keep the engine properly tuned and serviced and the tyres inflated to the right pressure. Avoid fast starts and sudden braking when driving. Combine trips where possible, do not carry unnecessary weight in the car, and switch the engine off if you are stuck in traffic for a long time. Ideally, walk or use public transport when you can.

FURTHER INFORMATION

Addresses

- **Building Research Establishment,** Bucknalls Lane, Garston, Watford WD2 7JR
(Tel. 01923 894040).
- **Council for Registered Gas Installers (CORGI),** 4 Elmwood, Chineham Business Park, Crockford Lane, Basingstoke, Hants RG24 8WG
(Tel. 01256 707060).
- **National Cavity Insulation Association,** P.O. Box 12, Haslemere, Surrey GU27 3AH
(Tel. 01428 654011).
- **Energy Action Grants Agency,** P.O. Box 1NG, Newcastle upon Tyne NE99 2RP
(Freefone 0800 181667).
- **Cavity Insulation Guarantee Agency,** 39 High Street, Redbourn, Herts AL3 7LW
(Tel. 01582 792283).

- **Energy Efficiency Office,** Department of the Environment, 2 Marsham Street, London SW1P 3EB.
(Tel. 0171 276 3791).
- **Glass and Glazing Federation,** 44–48 Borough High Street, London SE1 1XB
(Tel. 0171 403 7177).
- **Heating and Ventilating Contractors' Association,** 34 Palace Court, London W2 4JG
(Tel. 0171 229 2488).
- **Neighbourhood Energy Action,** St. Andrew's House, 90–92 Pilgrim Street, Newcastle upon Tyne NE1 6SG
(Tel. 0191 261 5677).
- **Local Energy Advice Centres**
(Tel. 0800 512012).
- **Wasting Energy Costs the Earth campaign**
(Tel. 0345 86 86 86 for free information pack).

Births •

Marriage •

Divorce and separation •

Rights in other relationships •

Death •

Social security and the family •

Child care •

Births

Action on becoming pregnant • Maternity certificate • Maternity leave •
Maternity benefits • Health and dental care • Registration of birth • Stillbirths •
Further information

- **WHAT DO I DO WHEN I BECOME PREGNANT?** You should visit
  your GP/midwife as soon as you can to confirm your pregnancy. He or she
  will advise on what tests you should have and why, and will help you decide
  the type of antenatal care best suited to you. If your GP does not offer
  maternity care, or you would prefer to go to a different practitioner, you
  can transfer to another doctor for maternity care alone, returning to your
  original doctor after the birth. The family health services authority
  (FHSA) will advise you: see your local phone book. Alternatively, you can
  obtain maternity care from a hospital, have shared care from a hospital
  and GP together, or ask the head of midwifery services at your local maternity unit to arrange home care by a midwife only. Almost all babies are
  born in hospital, where full medical facilities are available, but you are
  entitled to a home birth if you want one. It is a good idea in any event to
  attend a course of antenatal classes to help prepare you and your partner
  for the arrival of the baby.

- **MATERNITY CERTIFICATE** At 14 weeks before your baby is due,
  your doctor or midwife will issue you with a maternity
  certificate (*form MAT B1*), showing the date your baby is due. You will need
  to provide this certificate when you apply for certain types of maternity
  benefit.

- **WHAT DO I DO IF I AM WORKING?** Once your pregnancy is confirmed, you should inform your employer in writing. Your employer must
  allow you reasonable time off from work, with pay, for antenatal care and
  you are entitled to 14 weeks' maternity leave from work. Your employer

will tell you whether you are entitled to Statutory Maternity Pay (SMP), which is a weekly payment from your employer paid while you are off work having the baby, provided you satisfy certain criteria (see also under Employment on p. 68). If you are entitled to SMP, your employer will normally retain your maternity certificate for the duration of your maternity leave.

During maternity leave you are entitled to all your normal terms and conditions of employment except for monetary wages or salary. If you have more than two years' continuous service with your employer you can also choose to return to work after a longer period of maternity absence lasting up to 28 weeks after the week in which the baby is born. Some employers may have agreements under which maternity pay and leave are better than the legally-required/statutory minimum. Some employers may also offer paternity leave to prospective fathers.

As a prospective mother you should give your employer at least three weeks' notice in writing of the date you intend to start maternity leave and of the expected week the baby is due. If you plan to take advantage of the right to the longer period of maternity absence, you must notify your employer at this stage that this is your intention.

- **WHAT OTHER MATERNITY BENEFITS ARE AVAILABLE?** If you do not qualify for Statutory Maternity Pay – for example, because you have recently given up your job, or changed jobs, or have recently become self-employed – you may be able to get up to 18 weeks' maternity allowance from the Department of Social Security. To claim Maternity Allowance fill in *form MA1*, which you can get from your local social security office, and send it in not more than 14 weeks before the week the baby is due. You will need to include your maternity certificate.

If you or your partner are getting Income Support, Family Credit or Disability Working Allowance (see p. 58), you may be eligible for a one-off Maternity Payment from the Social Fund. Ask at your local social security office for claim *form SF100*.

- **FREE DENTAL TREATMENT AND NHS PRESCRIPTIONS** You qualify automatically for free NHS dental treatment while you are pregnant (provided you were pregnant at the start of the treatment) and for a year after your baby's birth. See *leaflet D11 NHS Dental Treatment*. You can also get free NHS prescriptions while you are pregnant and for a year after the birth. To claim free prescriptions, get *form FW8* from your doctor, midwife or health visitor and send it, when completed, to your nearest family health services authority. You will then receive an exemption form.

- **HOW DO I REGISTER THE BIRTH?** You are legally obliged to register your baby's birth within 42 days of the birth. It may be possible to register the birth before you leave hospital: the hospital staff will advise you on this. If you do not register the birth while you are in hospital, or if you have had your baby at home, you can register the birth at the local Registrar's Office (see in the local phone book under Registration of Births, Deaths and Marriages). You can also give details of your baby's birth at any other Registrar's Office for onward transmission to the registrar for the area in which the birth occurred.

- **TWO-PARENT AND SINGLE-PARENT FAMILIES** If the baby's mother and father are married at the time of birth or conception, either parent can register the birth. If the parents are not married at the time of the baby's birth or conception, the father's details can only be entered into the Register in certain circumstances. If you are an unmarried mother you are not normally obliged to give details of the father for inclusion in the entry. If the father's details are not entered at the time of registration, it may be possible for this to be done at a later date.

- **INFORMATION REQUIRED BY THE REGISTRAR** You will need to supply the registrar with the following information: the date and place of the baby's birth (and separate times for multiple births); the sex of the baby; the forenames and surname chosen for the child; if applicable, the father's forenames and surname, date and place of birth, and present occupation; the mother's forenames and surname, surname before marriage (if applicable), date and place of birth, address, occupation (optional), date of marriage (if applicable) and number of previous children.

- **WHAT SHOULD I BE GIVEN?** You will be issued with a short birth certificate free of charge. This short certificate meets most ordinary needs but a full birth certificate – that is, a copy of the full entry in the register is also obtainable. The registrar will also give you *form FP58*, so that your baby can be registered with a doctor. Fill in the form and either take or send it to your doctor, who will forward it to your family health services authority. The authority will then send you an NHS card with your baby's number on it.

● **WHAT HAPPENS IF MY BABY IS STILLBORN?** If your baby is stillborn (that is, born dead after the 24th week of pregnancy), your entitlement to free prescriptions and dental treatment, SMP, Maternity Allowance and a Maternity Payment from the Social Fund (see p. 37) does not change. The doctor or midwife will give you a medical certificate of stillbirth which you should give to the registrar (see also p. 51). If no doctor or midwife was present at the birth, ask the registrar for declaration form 35. Having filled it in, give it back to the registrar who will then give you a certificate of burial.

FURTHER INFORMATION

• The Patient's Charter sets out the standards you should expect from the NHS maternity service and explains your rights as a 'consumer'. It also tells you what you can do if you are dissatisfied with the service provided.

• Information on SMP, maternity leave and other benefits is given in the leaflet A guide to maternity benefits (NI17A), available from your local social security office. Further information on birth registration is provided in leaflet 362: Registering your baby's birth – A guide for parents (available from your local Registrar of Births), or you can telephone the **General Register Office** (0151 471 4805). Other useful contact points include the **National Childbirth Trust** (Tel. 0181 992 8637), the **Maternity Alliance** (Tel. 0171 837 1265) and the **British Pregnancy Advisory Service** (Tel. 01564 793226).

Marriage

Qualifications for marriage • Civil ceremonies • Church of England marriages • Marriages outside the Church of England • Documentation, witnesses and fees

- **WHO CAN BE MARRIED?** Any two people can get married provided that:
- both are at least 16 years of age on the day of the marriage (and the consent of parent or lawful guardian has been given if either is under 18);
- they are not related to each other in a way that would prevent their marriage (a register office will supply a full list);
- they are at present unmarried;
- they are capable of understanding the marriage ceremony and of consenting to the marriage; and
- they are male and female respectively.

- **WHAT TYPES OF MARRIAGE ARE AVAILABLE?** You can be married by a religious ceremony or by a civil ceremony. A religious marriage, whether Christian or non-Christian, must take place in the presence of a minister, clergyman, pastor, priest, registrar or other person legally entitled to register the marriage. A civil marriage may only be solemnised in the presence of a superintendent registrar and registrar of marriages.

- **MARRIAGE BY CIVIL CEREMONY** The Marriage Act 1994 enabled a superintendent registrar to issue a certificate or licence (see p. 41) for a marriage in a register office outside the couple's district(s) of residence. Couples were previously restricted to having the ceremony in the register office for the area in which they lived. The Marriage Act 1994 also widened the choice of venue for a civil marriage to include any other suitable premises such as stately homes or hotels which are approved for marriage by the local authority.

For couples marrying by certificate, notice must be given by one of the couple to the superintendent registrar of the district where they have a seven-day residential qualification. If they live in different districts notice must be given to both superintendent registrars, and there is a waiting period of 21 days before the marriage can take place.

Where the marriage is to be by licence, notice must be given to the superintendent registrar of the district where there is a 15-day residential qualification. The marriage can then take place after one day (not Sunday, Good Friday or Christmas Day).

- **MARRIAGE IN THE CHURCH OF ENGLAND** A Church of England (or of Wales) marriage may take place after one of the following preliminaries:

- publication of the banns (or notice of marriage);

- the issue of an ecclesiastical (or 'common') licence;

- the issue of a special licence; or

- the issue of a superintendent registrar's certificate.

In a Church of England (or of Wales) marriage there is no need to enter into the civil preliminaries associated with register office marriages and with those of other denominations and faiths.

Publication of the banns

Speak to the local clergy of the parish in which you live and he or she will advise you on the procedure. Banns must be published on three Sundays before the marriage can take place.

Common licence

This exempts the couple from having to publish banns (see above). Application should be made to the Diocesan Registrar. Your parish clergy will advise you on how to go about obtaining such a licence.

Special licence

Special licences, enabling a marriage to take place legally according to the rites of the Church of England (or of Wales) at any time and place, are issued only in serious emergencies or very exceptional circumstances. Application should be made to the Registrar of the Court of Faculties (1 The Sanctuary, London SW1P 3JT).

Superintendent registrar's certificate

A marriage according to the rites of the Church of England (or of Wales) may take place on the authority of a certificate of a superintendent registrar instead of after the publication of banns. *Form 357* issued by the General Register Office (and available from your local register office) explains the conditions attached to this certificate.

- **MARRIAGE OUTSIDE THE CHURCH OF ENGLAND** The procedure for marrying in a religious denomination or faith other than the Church of England (or of Wales) is the same as that for marriage in a register office, except that the ceremony must take place (a) at the location specified in the superintendent registrar's authority (that is, a place of religious worship that has been officially registered for marriages by the Registrar General); and (b) in the presence of a registrar of marriages or an authorised person (that is, a member of a particular community appointed by a religious body and approved by the Registrar General), who will register the marriage and issue a marriage certificate.

- **DOCUMENTATION, WITNESSES AND FEES** You may be asked to produce a copy of your birth certificate. If you have been married before you will also be asked to produce documentary evidence of the dissolution of your previous marriage or of the death of your former spouse. You must arrange for the attendance of two witnesses at the marriage ceremony, wherever it is held, so that they can sign the marriage register. A certified copy of the entry recording the marriage may be obtained at the time of the marriage.

Full details of the fees payable for a register office marriage are contained in *form 357A* available from your local Registrar of Births, Deaths and Marriages. Your local clergy or other celebrant will advise you on fees payable for religious wedding ceremonies. The fees payable in all parishes in England and Wales are set out in *leaflet 357B*.

Divorce and separation

Grounds for divorce • Pros and cons of using a solicitor • Initiating proceedings • Court procedures • Decree nisi and decree absolute • Arrangements for children • Judicial separation

Divorce is a very serious step to take and can have a profound effect on those involved. The procedure to obtain a divorce is relatively easy, but many people make the mistake of thinking that once the divorce decree is awarded their problems are over. Difficulties faced by couples are frequently about money, housing and children. These are difficult problems to deal with at the best of times, let alone when couples may also be coping with the intense emotions that separation and divorce often entail.

- **MAKING THE DECISION** If you have decided that you wish to divorce, you have to be sure that you can prove to a court that you have legitimate grounds for saying that the marriage is at an end. If the court is to find that the marriage has 'irretrievably broken down', it will require proof or admission of one or more of the following grounds:

- that your spouse has committed adultery;

- that your spouse's behaviour has been so unreasonable that you can no longer bear to live with him/her;

- that you and your spouse have lived apart for at least two years and that he/she agrees to a divorce; or

- that you and your spouse have lived apart for at least five years, whether he/she agrees to a divorce or not.

In England and Wales you cannot start a petition for divorce unless you have been married for a year or more. You must also demonstrate that you and your spouse have been permanently domiciled within the United Kingdom for at least a year prior to the start of the petition.

- **WILL I NEED A SOLICITOR?** Do-it-yourself divorce is relatively easy if you and your spouse agree that there should be a divorce and on what basis. But you will probably find it useful to obtain some legal advice before starting your petition if:

- you are uncertain whether you have grounds;

- your spouse is not likely to agree to a divorce;

- there are likely to be disputes about property and/or maintenance; or

- you have children.

In the last respect, the crucial issues are whether you and your spouse are in agreement on which of you the children should live with, on adequate contact for the other parent, and on what provisions are envisaged for the financial support of the children.

Even if you are in agreement with your spouse on such matters, a solicitor may be able to put your agreement into a form of words that a judge will find acceptable, or to point out things that you have overlooked. If you do decide to consult a solicitor, choose one who is experienced in matrimonial work – perhaps a member of the Solicitors' Family Law Association, which has a code of practice designed to help parties to reach amicable settlements. Your local Citizens Advice Bureau or library will have copies of the Law Society's lists of local solicitors and their specialities. Before retaining the services of a solicitor you should ask about the likely costs and also ask yourself what you want to achieve, so that you can use such services efficiently and economically. Although legal aid is generally no longer available to finance an undefended divorce suit, it may be available for ancillary matters if there is reason to believe that the application will be opposed. Remember that the higher the legal costs, the less money there will be to share between you, your spouse and any children.

If you decide to handle the divorce yourself, the court will give you the necessary forms and tell you what to do next. The forms are free. Remember that court staff are not solicitors: they are not qualified to give legal advice or to answer questions about, for example, financial support, grounds for divorce or division of property. If you need help with filling in the forms, your local Citizens Advice Bureau will advise.

- **HOW DO I START A DIVORCE PETITION?** You can start your petition in any divorce county court or in the Principal Registry in London. Addresses and telephone numbers of such courts are listed in your local telephone directory under Courts. The court will tell you what the fees are and how to pay. (If you think you may be exempt from such fees, fill in *form D92*.)

You will need to prepare at least three copies of the divorce petition (*form D8*) and, if you have children, three copies of the statement of arrangements for the children (*form D8A*). One copy of these forms is for you to keep, one copy is for the court and one copy will be sent by the court to your spouse (the respondent). If you are petitioning for divorce on grounds of your spouse's adultery with someone named in your petition, you will also need a copy of the petition for that person (the co-respondent). The notes accompanying *form D8* will help you to complete your petition.

- **WHAT IS THE NEXT STEP?** Once you have sent in the relevant forms you will be sent a notice of issue of petition (*form D9H*), which will tell you when the petition was sent to the respondent (and any co-respondent). This will be done by the court with an acknowledgment of service (*form D10*), including a copy of the proposed arrangements for any children. The notice of issue will also tell you what to do if the respondent (or any co-respondent) does not reply to your petition. They have eight days to return the acknowledgment of service.

Contested divorce petitions are rare these days: there are powerful financial and other reasons for avoiding such confrontation in the courts, and in any case the law allows divorce without consent after five years of separation. Assuming the respondent does not contest your petition, you can apply to the court for 'directions for trial' (*form D84*), at which point you should also submit an affidavit of evidence (*form D80*). The court staff will pass the papers with your case file to the divorce court judge.

- **WILL I HAVE TO ATTEND COURT HEARINGS?** If there is no dispute between you and your spouse, you may not have to attend the court hearing that will consider your divorce petition. But you may have to attend if you are requesting an order for financial support or are in dispute with your spouse over custody of children.

- **HOW IS A DIVORCE GRANTED?** If the judge finds no objection to your petition, he or she will grant a divorce in the form of a decree nisi (*form D29*), which is the first of two decrees that you must have before you are finally divorced and free to re-marry. A decree nisi means that the divorce will become final unless something arises to the contrary in the interim. The minimum interval between the granting of a decree nisi and a decree absolute is six weeks. In other words, the first date on which you can apply for a decree absolute (using *form D36*) is six weeks and one day from the date of the pronouncement of the decree nisi. If everything is in order, the court will send you and the respondent a decree absolute (*form D37*).

- **CHILDREN AND DIVORCE** Divorce is a decision reached by adults but often has a profound effect on children. Questions of fundamental importance are what financial provision is being made for the children and how they are going to keep in contact with the parent with whom they will not be living. One of the family conciliation services may be able to help you and your partner find common ground and mutually acceptable solutions in respect of arrangements for children if a divorce is in prospect (your local Citizens Advice Bureau will have addresses). If you cannot reach a satisfactory agreement, the court will make a ruling on the contentious issues.

- **JUDICIAL SEPARATION** At any time after marriage a husband or wife can ask a court for a decree of judicial separation. This means that the marriage is not legally dissolved but that the two partners agree to live apart, and can ask the court to make provisions for property or maintenance. The procedure is similar to that for divorce, except that there is no interim stage.

Rights in other relationships

The home • Children and maintenance • Inheritance • Benefits and taxation

• **LEGAL RIGHTS** The law in England and Wales does not recognise common law marriage and consequently the legal rights of an unmarried couple are considerably different from those of a married couple.

What happens to the family home when an unmarried couple break up?

If an unmarried couple's relationship breaks down and the name of only one partner is on the title deeds, lease or rent book of the family home, that partner alone is the owner in accordance with the law.

Is it possible to dispute ownership if property is in one name only?

If the property is in one name it is only in exceptional circumstances that the person whose name is not on the title deeds can claim a share in its value. To prove that the property was jointly owned, even though not on the title deeds, the person disputing ownership would have to prove, for example, that they paid the deposit or mortgage repayments or that they had done a great deal of work on the property and made a significant contribution to increasing its value. There are other grounds that may be used for establishing a claim and it is best to seek legal advice for each individual case. If the claim is not upheld, the person disputing ownership can be evicted. The court will give them a personal licence (permission) to live in the owner's home and the owner can end this permission by giving a reasonable notice to leave. The reasonable period of notice is a minimum of 28 days. If the woman has children the court may extend the period for six months. A woman with children who is given notice may make a claim against the man for a transfer of the home under the Children Act 1989.

What happens if the property is in joint names?

If the property is in joint names then generally the couple will be considered joint owners. If one part-owner feels that they are entitled to more than 50 per cent, they can apply to the court under the Law of Property Act 1925. If one part-owner wants to sell the property and the other part-owner doesn't, the former can generally insist that the property is sold and apply to court for a court order against the ex-partner who doesn't want to sell.

On certain occasions the court may decide that the property should remain a family home until the youngest child is 18. If there are any other assets, a share cannot be automatically claimed by an ex-partner; they are only entitled to what is legally theirs.

What happens if the property is rented?

The lawful tenant of a rented property is the person whose name is on the rent book or lease. If there is only one name then the sole tenant can evict the other tenant after giving notice. The sole tenant can also surrender the tenancy to the landlord without first having to offer it to the ex-partner. If the sole tenant abandons the rented property, the tenant who remains does not have the right to stay on in the property without the landlord's agreement and the landlord is able to apply to the court for an eviction notice. If a woman without tenancy has children she may be able to make a claim to stay on under the Children Act 1989. Joint tenancies are complicated to sort out and legal advice should be taken for individual cases. Different categories of tenancy have different degrees of protection afforded by the law (see p. 13).

Who has responsibility for the children?

If a couple are not married the woman has sole parental responsibility in law for their children (see p. 60). This means that the mother alone has the legal right to make decisions concerning the children. The unmarried father can gain parental responsibility either through agreement with the mother or by successfully applying to the court for a parental responsibility order. A child of unmarried parents cannot acquire British citizenship through his or her father.

Can an unmarried ex-partner claim maintenance?
When an unmarried couple break up neither partner is entitled to claim maintenance for themselves. Maintenance to provide for children is now assessed and collected by the Child Support Agency.

Does an unmarried partner have the right to inherit the other partner's estate?
The unmarried partner will only inherit the deceased partner's estate if there is a clear will. Without a will the surviving partner has no right to inherit any part of the estate, which automatically goes to the deceased's relatives. The remaining partner may be able to make a claim if he or she was financially dependent on the deceased but this could be a long and expensive process.

Are an unmarried couple entitled to the same benefits as a married couple?
An unmarried couple's entitlement to the benefits of state pension and maternity grant and allowance are assessed only on their own National Insurance contributions and they cannot take their partner's contributions into account as can a married couple. An unmarried woman is not entitled to widow's benefits.

How does being unmarried affect the way a couple are taxed?
Unmarried couples can claim only their single person's tax allowance and they are assessed separately for income tax. An unmarried parent has an additional personal allowance but only one allowance for each family is permitted. The transfer of property between an unmarried couple may be liable for capital gains tax and unmarried couples are not exempt from paying inheritance tax on their deceased partner's will. Mortgage interest relief applies to a residence and not to an individual borrower, so unmarried couples do not gain double tax relief.

Death

Initial action • Registration • Funerals • The coroner • Post mortems and inquests • Organ donation • Wills and the estate • Telling others

• **WHAT DO I DO FIRST?** When a death occurs, medical evidence as to the cause must be given. If a death occurs at home and was expected, you should contact the doctor who attended the dead person (the deceased) during their last illness. If the doctor can confirm the cause of death, he or she will give you a (free) medical certificate of the cause of death as well as guidance on how to get the death registered (which you have to do by law).

In the case of a sudden or unexpected death, call the family doctor or telephone for the emergency ambulance service (999). If you think that the death was accidental, violent or suspicious in any way, then call the police as well and don't disturb anything before they arrive. The death may be referred to the coroner (see p. 52).

If the death occurs in hospital, the staff (or the police, following an accident) will contact you and issue the death certificate. You will need to go to the hospital to collect the deceased's belongings and, if he or she was not already an in-patient, to identify the body. The hospital mortuary will hold the body until you can make arrangements for it to be taken away.

• **HOW DO I REGISTER THE DEATH?** By law every death must be registered by the registrar of births and deaths for the area in which it happened. The address will be in the phone book under Registration of Births, Deaths and Marriages. If the death has been referred to the coroner, it cannot be registered until the coroner says so. If the death has not been referred, you should go to the registrar as soon as possible – in any case within five days.

Take along the papers that you have been given by the doctor or coroner. You will need to tell the registrar the personal details of the deceased (name, address, occupation, date and place of birth), the date and place of death, and your relationship to the deceased. You will also be asked whether the deceased was getting any state benefits and the date of birth of any surviving spouse.

What should I be given?
The registrar will give you a certificate to bury or cremate the body (unless the coroner has issued one already). This has to be given to the funeral director before burial or cremation can take place. You will also be given a certificate of registration of death, which you may need for social security purposes, and leaflets on welfare benefits.

The death certificate is a certified copy of the entry in the death register. You are likely to need at least one copy, for example for getting grant of probate (see p. 54) or for any pension claims. The registrar can give you a copy or copies, but you will be charged a fee. Some organisations may accept a photocopy of a death certificate, whereas others may insist upon a separate certified copy, which they may or may not return to you.

Registering stillbirths
When registering a stillbirth (a child born dead after the 24th week of pregnancy), the registrar needs a certificate of stillbirth signed by the attending doctor or midwife. If no doctor or midwife was present at the birth, or examined the body, one of the parents or some other qualified informant can make a declaration on a special form available from the registrar.

● **HOW DO I ARRANGE THE FUNERAL?** Before you make final funeral arrangements, make sure that the death does not have to be referred to the coroner, as this may affect the date when the body can be released for burial or cremation.

Most funerals are arranged by a funeral director or undertaker. It's advisable to choose one who belongs to the National Association of Funeral

Directors (Tel. 0121 711 1343). A basic funeral includes a coffin, a hearse and one following car up to a stated mileage, bearers to carry the coffin, and the services of the undertaker. It does not include things like burial or crematorium fees, flowers or notices in the press.

Who pays?

Some people insure during their lifetime for their funeral or contribute to schemes to cover the expenses. Usually the cost is paid out of the deceased's estate (money and property he or she left), although the assets may not be immediately available. Some institutions, for example building societies, may be prepared to release up to £5,000 worth of assets on the evidence of the death certificate alone, although they are not bound to do so.

If you are on a low income and need help with funeral costs, you may be able to get help from the Social Security Social Fund (look in the phone book under Social Security). Payments from the Social Fund have to be paid back out of the estate of the deceased. If no-one is able or willing to arrange and pay for the funeral, the local council or health authority may do so, but only where the funeral has not already been arranged.

Cremation or burial?

Check the deceased's will (if there is one) for any instructions regarding the funeral. It is up to the executor of the will (see p. 54) or nearest relative to decide whether the body is to be buried or cremated.

If the deceased is to be buried, look through their papers to see if a plot in a churchyard or cemetery has already been organised. If not, a plot will have to be bought. The funeral director will provide details. More forms need to be filled in for a cremation than for a burial.

- **WHEN DOES THE CORONER NEED TO BE INFORMED?** A doctor or registrar will report a person's death to the local coroner (a qualified doctor or lawyer) if the death was sudden and unexplained, or if it might have been due to violence or to an accident. The coroner must also be informed if the deceased was not attended by a doctor during the last illness, or if the certifying doctor did not see the deceased within 14 days of death or after death, or if death might have resulted from an industrial disease.

If the coroner decides that there is no need for further investigation, the death can be registered from the certificate provided by the doctor. In some instances, however, the coroner may think that the cause of death must be looked into further. The death cannot then be registered until a notification is provided by the coroner after his or her inquiries have been completed. The funeral will have to await the outcome of any such investigations.

- **WHEN DOES THE CORONER ORDER A POST MORTEM OR OPEN AN INQUEST?** If a relative's death resulted from a natural illness, but the doctors want to find out more about the cause, you may be asked for your permission to carry out a post mortem examination of the body. If it is not clear to the coroner that death was due to a natural cause, he or she will normally arrange for an examination of the body to be made. Your consent is not needed in these circumstances. The post mortem examination will often show that death was due to natural causes. In such a case, there is no inquest. Instead the coroner will send a certificate to the registrar of deaths so that the death can be registered.

If the coroner is unable to establish that the death was due to natural causes, or if the death occurred in prison, the coroner is obliged by law to hold an inquest. Every inquest – except those which involve national security – is held in public. The purpose of an inquest is to ascertain the identity of the deceased, the circumstances of the death and the details needed to enable the death to be registered.

- **WHAT ABOUT DONATION OF BODY ORGANS FOR TRANSPLANT?** If the deceased had expressed an objection to the removal and use of any of his or her organs after death, you cannot agree to their donation. In cases where consent has been given, the heart, liver and kidneys must be removed within half an hour of death so they cannot normally be used if the death occurs at home.

If the death has to be reported to the coroner, his or her consent may be necessary before the organs can be donated. A medical certificate must be issued before any organs can be removed.

Some people wish to donate their whole body after death for medical teaching purposes. Where this is the case, a signed statement making this request will usually have been left with the deceased's will or personal papers. This should give the address and telephone number to be contacted. If the person lived in London, it will be the London Anatomy Office (Tel. 0181 846 1216). Outside London or the home counties the contact number will be that of the nearest medical school. In case of doubt or difficulty, phone HM Inspector of Anatomy (Tel. 0171 972 4342).

- **WHAT HAPPENS TO THE PROPERTY AND POSSESSIONS?** If you have to deal with everything owned by the deceased, you are known as the personal representative (also known as the executor if you are named in the will, or the administrator if there is no will). If there is a will, it will say what should happen to the deceased's property and possessions – the estate. You will be responsible for paying, from the proceeds of the estate, all the deceased's debts, taxes and expenses, including funeral costs. After these liabilities have been settled, you can share out the rest of the estate to the beneficiaries.

  If there is a will, you need to apply for a grant of probate (unless the sum involved is very small), which gives you legal permission to pay the bills and deal with the estate. You can get advice from a probate registry office (look under that title in the phone book) or Citizens Advice Bureau. You may do this yourself, but some people prefer to employ a solicitor and charge his or her fees to the estate.

  If there isn't a will, as the administrator you have to distribute the estate among the relatives according to rules of entitlement. These are explained in a DSS booklet entitled *What to do after a Death* (*leaflet D49*) available from your local social security office.

- **WHO DO I NEED TO TELL?** Depending on individual circumstances, the following people or organisations may need to be told about the death:
  - the solicitor dealing with the affairs of the deceased;
  - the local social services and housing departments;
  - family doctor/hospital;
  - the Inland Revenue;
  - the social security office;
  - employer/trade union;

- school or college;
- gas, electricity, telephone and water services;
- banks, building societies and insurance companies;
- Passport Office;
- driving licence centre (DVLA);
- clubs and associations;
- the post office.

Social security and the family

Income Support • Family Credit • Housing Benefit • Council Tax Benefit • Social Fund • Benefits for parents and children • Sick, injured and disabled people's benefits • Retirement pension • Death benefits • Further information

The social security system is designed to secure a basic standard of living for people in financial need by providing income during periods of inability to earn, help for families and assistance with costs arising from disability. Your entitlement to receive some benefits depends on your having already paid, or been credited with, enough National Insurance contributions. Other benefits are non-contributory and do not depend on the payment of National Insurance contributions. A wide range of benefits is available; the most commonly received are described in this section.

- **INCOME SUPPORT** Income Support is a benefit to help people aged 18 or over whose income is below a certain level. It can be paid to top up other benefits (including Unemployment Benefit – see p. 70), earnings from part-time work including self-employed work, or if you have no money at all coming in. Your right to Income Support does not depend on National Insurance contributions.

To get Income Support you must normally be available for work and show that you are taking reasonable steps to find a job (unless you are sick, disabled, a lone parent, 60 or over, getting Invalid Care Allowance or pregnant). You cannot normally get Income Support if you or your partner are working for an average of 16 hours or more a week. People with savings or capital worth more than £8,000 are not eligible for income benefit; savings between £3,000 and £8,000 will reduce the amount received.

The amount you get on Income Support will depend, among other things, on your age, whether you have a partner, and whether you have any dependent children, disabilities or savings.

• **FAMILY CREDIT** Family Credit is a tax-free benefit for working families with children. It is not dependent on National Insurance contributions. If you get Family Credit, you and your family will also get help with NHS costs, for example, for prescriptions and dental treatment.

To be eligible for Family Credit you must be responsible for at least one child under 16 (or under 19 if in full-time education). You or your partner must be working at least 16 hours a week and not have savings above a certain amount (see under Income Support on p. 56). You can get Family Credit whether you are employed or self-employed, a couple or a lone parent. For more information, you can call the Family Credit Helpline on 01253 50 00 50.

• **HOUSING BENEFIT** Housing Benefit is a tax-free benefit paid by local councils to people who need help to pay their rent (including hotel, guest house or hostel charges). It does not cover mortgage charges, but you may get help with mortgage interest in your payments if you get Income Support (see p. 56). Your right to Housing Benefit does not depend on National Insurance contributions and is available equally to employed, self-employed, unemployed and retired people. You don't have to be in receipt of Income Support, but savings above a certain amount will affect your entitlement to Housing Benefit.

If you do get Income Support and pay rent, you will usually qualify for maximum Housing Benefit. If you do not get Income Support, you will still qualify for Housing Benefit (possibly the maximum) if the money you have coming in is less than the amount calculated as sufficient for your needs, given your personal circumstances (including number of children).

• **COUNCIL TAX BENEFIT** The council tax is the tax set by local authorities to help pay for services. Most owner-occupiers or tenants have to pay council tax but you may be able to get help if you need it. Nearly all the rules which apply to Housing Benefit (see above) apply to Council Tax Benefit. The amount you will get will depend on your income, savings and personal circumstances. In some situations all of your council tax will be paid.

- **SOCIAL FUND** The Social Fund helps people with expenses which are difficult to meet out of ordinary income. Benefits available include:

- maternity payments, which may be up to £100 to help buy things for a new baby;

- funeral payments, which are for people on low incomes who need help with funeral costs (see p. 52);

- cold weather payments, which are non-discretionary payments to help with the cost of heating during very cold weather; payments are automatically sent to pensioners on Income Support when the mean daily temperature is equal to or below 0° Celsius for seven consecutive days;

- community care grants, which help people in certain priority groups, like the elderly or disabled, to lead independent lives in the community;

- budgeting loans, which are made to people on Income Support to cover important occasional expenses (buying a cooker, for example); and

- crisis loans, which provide help to cover immediate short-term expenses in an emergency or following a disaster, where there is a serious risk to the health or safety of a family.

Some of these payments are repayable loans; others do not have to be repaid. Most are available only to people receiving other types of benefit and any savings the claimant has will generally be taken into account.

- **BENEFITS FOR PARENTS AND CHILDREN** In addition to the various maternity benefits (see p. 37), a number of other benefits are available to help with bringing up children. Child Benefit is a tax-free weekly cash payment for nearly everyone who is responsible for a child under 16 (or under 19 if in full-time education up to A-level standard). One Parent Benefit is a tax-free weekly cash payment on top of Child Benefit for certain people who are bringing up a child alone, payable for the eldest child only, regardless of income or National Insurance contributions. Guardian's Allowance is also a tax-free weekly cash benefit, on top of Child Benefit, which may be payable if you are bringing up a child who has lost both parents, whether or not you are the legal guardian. Sometimes it can be paid even if one of the child's parents is still alive.

All children under 16 get free NHS prescriptions, free dental treatment, free eye tests and vouchers towards the cost of glasses. Your local education welfare office can provide help with children's clothing and with the cost of keeping a child at school beyond the age of 16.

- **SICK, INJURED AND DISABLED PEOPLE'S BENEFITS** Most people who work for an employer and are sick for at least four days in a row can get Statutory Sick Pay (SSP) from their employers for a maximum of 28 weeks in any spell or series of linked spells of sickness. From April 1995 there is a single rate of SSP for all qualifying employees provided their average weekly earnings are at least equivalent to the lower earnings limit for the payment of National Insurance contributions. Your employer will pay your SSP in the same way as your wages.

  If you are employed and incapable of work and cannot get SSP from your employer, or you are self-employed, unemployed or non-employed, you may be able to get Incapacity Benefit, which replaced sickness benefit and invalidity benefit in April 1995. (For details of disability benefits see p. 97.)

- **RETIREMENT PENSION** The retirement pension is a taxable weekly benefit for people who have reached pensionable age (65 for men, 60 for women and meet the National Insurance contributions conditions (see p. 114).

- **DEATH BENEFITS** In addition to a funeral payment from the Social Fund (see p. 52), which is payable to many categories of benefit claimant, surviving wives may also be entitled to a Widow's Payment, a Widowed Mother's Allowance or a Widow's Pension.

FURTHER INFORMATION

A comprehensive guide to social security and NHS benefits is published by the Benefits Agency in the free booklet Which Benefit? Your local social security office (listed in the phone book under Social Security or Benefits Agency,) will have a copy, as well as other leaflets explaining who is eligible for which benefit and advising how claims should be made.

Child care

Parents and children • Children in need • Day care for children •
Children looked after away from home • Adoption

- **PARENTS AND CHILDREN** The law provides a collection of rights, powers and duties to parents. The Children Act 1989 refers to these collectively as 'parental responsibility', the exercise of which is left largely to parents subject to two limitations. First, the criminal law imposes penalties if minimal standards of care are not maintained. The civil law provides for the protection of children from harm and neglect by their parents and others. Second, parental responsibility diminishes as a child gains sufficient understanding to take his or her own decisions.

  Other than through an adoption order there is no legal or administrative means by which a parent's responsibility can be taken away permanently. There may be occasions due to adverse circumstances, however, where these responsibilities are restricted and have to be shared with others for the time being.

  Where parents are married, they each have parental responsibility for their child. Otherwise the mother alone has parental responsibility, unless the father acquires it either by a court order or by formal agreement with the mother. Although a father may not have parental responsibility, he will be liable to provide financial support for his child.

- **CHILDREN IN NEED** Each local government authority has a duty to promote the welfare of children in need. So far as possible, services provided for children in need should be aimed at keeping such children within their families. According to needs, services provided may include counselling, practical help in the home, social activities, day care and –

exceptionally – accommodation for a child away from his or her family home.

- **DAY CARE FOR CHILDREN** Local authorities are required to provide day care for children in need who are aged five years and under and not yet at school, if their particular needs require this service. They may also provide day care and supervised activities for young children who have not been assessed as 'in need'. Otherwise parents may make their own arrangements for day care for their children in registered day care services or with registered child-minders. The local authority is required to maintain and make available a register of child-minders and people who provide day care services such as playgroups and day nurseries. Day care services are unlawful unless registered by the local authority as providing services which meet required standards.

- **CHILDREN LOOKED AFTER AWAY FROM HOME** Under the Children Act 1989, local authorities are required to provide accommodation for children whose parents, for whatever reason, are prevented from looking after them (or when a child has been abandoned). Generally such children are looked after under voluntary arrangements with their parents. Parents retain their parental responsibility, and a placement cannot be made in the face of parental objections unless the child is over 16 years of age.

Parents may also make private arrangements with other unrelated adults for their child to be fostered. In these circumstances, the parents have a duty to inform the local authority in advance of their plans to place their child; the foster parents are also under a duty to inform the local authority of their intention to receive the child. The authority must then visit the child and satisfy themselves that his or her welfare is satisfactory.

Local authorities must respond to information that a child may be suffering or at risk of significant harm. They have powers to seek a court order to protect the child. This may involve removal from home for a short period of not more than eight days in an emergency; for an interim period; or for any period up to the child's 18th birthday following a full court hearing. When a child is committed to the care of a local authority through care proceedings, the authority acquires parental responsibility. At the same time, according to the circumstances, the court may restrict the extent and nature of the contact which the child's parents may have with their child.

When a local authority places a child away from home, it should first enquire whether it is possible for a relative to provide accommodation. Practical help and financial assistance may be available. Failing this (and almost invariably in the case of children up to 12 years old), a local authority-approved foster home will be sought. The law requires the foster home to be located as close to the child's family home as possible, and for assistance to be provided for family members to maintain contact. For older children, particularly those with special needs, a place in a local authority community home or in an independent children's home may be sought. In each case, parents and the child (according to his or her age and level of understanding) will be involved in periodic reviews of the need for the child to continue to be accommodated away from home.

- **ADOPTION** Local authority social services departments are required by law to establish adoption services, provided in conjunction with approved voluntary adoption societies. These adoption services exist primarily to meet the needs of children who need permanent substitute families through adoption. The number of children, babies in particular, who are available for adoption is far exceeded by those people wishing to adopt. There is no legal right under the law to be considered for approval to adopt a child. In making an adoption order, the court's final consideration is for the welfare of the child.

In recent years, fewer than 7,000 children have been adopted annually. Of those, about half are adopted by one legal parent and a new partner, following marriage or remarriage. Under adoption law, it is unlawful to receive an unrelated child for adoption through an unapproved third party. Such children may only be placed by a local authority acting as an adoption agency or by an approved adoption society.

Adopters must be at least 21 years of age. Applications are restricted to married couples and single people. A successful application generally requires the free and unconditional agreement of each legal parent of the child.

In addition to finding adoptive homes and placing children for adoption, the adoption services can offer help and advice on a number of related issues. These include adoption allowances in the case of children with very special needs, and counselling for adults who were adopted and are seeking access to their original birth records.

Employment rights •

Employment service •

Redundancy •

Setting up a business/ •
self-employment

Safety at work •

Employment rights

Contract of employment • Employer's legal duties • Employee's legal duties •
Trade unions • Industrial action • Maternity • Equal opportunities • Equal pay •
Disability • Statutory Sick Pay • Further information

- **WHO IS AN EMPLOYEE?** An employee is someone who works for an
  employer under a contract of employment (contract of service). As an
  employee, you have a number of legal rights. Some of these come into
  effect as soon as you begin your employment, however many hours a week
  you work. For others you must have been employed for at least two years.

  In most cases it will be clear if you are an employee or self-employed. Where
  it is unclear, but you believe that you are an employee whose rights have
  been infringed, an industrial tribunal will decide (should you make a complaint about such infringement) whether or not you are an employee.

- **WHAT IS A CONTRACT OF EMPLOYMENT?** A contract of
  employment is an agreement between you and your employer. The contract may be oral, in writing or implied. Although the terms under which
  you are employed can be given informally, it is better to get them set out
  in detail at the start of your employment. This could save you practical and
  legal difficulties in the future. If you have been working for a month or
  more, then your employer must give you written information of the terms
  of your employment not later than two months after the start of your job.

- **WHAT SHOULD THE CONTRACT SAY?** Your contract must give
  the following information:

- your name, and your employer's name;

- your place of work (or, if you are required or allowed to work in more than
  one location, an indication of this and of your employer's address);

- the title or brief description of your job; the date when your employment (or continuous employment) started – including time worked for a previous employer where there has been a takeover or a transfer of business;

- your rate of pay, and any other financial benefits;

- the intervals of payment;

- the hours of work;

- any terms and conditions for holidays and holiday pay;

- the period of your employment if it is temporary;

- the details of the existence of any relevant collective agreements which affect the terms of your job;

- the terms and conditions of employment and payment if you are expected to work outside the United Kingdom for more than a month;

- the length of notice you have to give and are entitled to receive;

- entitlement to sick leave, including any sick pay entitlement; and

- any terms and conditions for pensions.

Your contract cannot be changed unless you agree to any changes your employer proposes, or unless there is a clause in the contract which allows the employer to change the terms unilaterally. The changes must be set out in full.

- **WHAT ARE MY EMPLOYER'S LEGAL DUTIES?** Your employer must:

- pay you according to the terms of your contract – in addition to Statutory Sick Pay, you may also be entitled to contractual sick pay if you are off work because of sickness or injury and if this is provided for in your contract;

- take reasonable care of your health and safety; and

- comply with his contractual obligations and statutory requirements (for example, to provide an itemised pay statement).

- **WHAT ARE MY LEGAL DUTIES?** You must:

- carry out lawful and reasonable orders given by your employer;

- not impede your employer's business;

- be loyal to your employer, by not setting yourself up in competition or disclosing confidential information about your employer's business; and

- take reasonable care in carrying out your work.

- **AM I ALLOWED TO BE A MEMBER OF A TRADE UNION?** It is unlawful for an employer to deny employment to individuals because they are (or are not) trade union members. It is also unlawful for an employer to dismiss, or take action short of dismissal against, employees on these grounds. This applies regardless of hours of work and length of service.

- **AM I ALLOWED TIME OFF FOR TRADE UNION ACTIVITIES?** Employers must let employees who are members of an independent recognised union take reasonable time off during working hours for union activities – excluding industrial action. Employers must also let employees who are lay officials of an independent recognised union take reasonable time off to carry out certain trade union duties and to undergo training relevant to those duties.

- **CAN I TAKE INDUSTRIAL ACTION?** You cannot be prevented from withdrawing your labour. But if you do so, you may be in breach of your employment contract and you may be dismissed. The organisation of industrial action is protected provided certain conditions are met. For example, the action must be in contemplation or furtherance of a trade dispute, as defined by law, and, if organised by a trade union, must be approved in a postal ballot and properly notified to the employer.

- **WHAT MATERNITY RIGHTS DO WOMEN HAVE?** A pregnant employee normally has the right to time off during working hours to attend an antenatal appointment. A woman suspended for health and safety reasons whilst pregnant or breastfeeding will normally be entitled to be paid by her employer. It is unfair to dismiss a woman because she is pregnant, during her pregnancy or maternity leave period.

Pregnant employees have a right to 14 weeks' maternity leave regardless of their length of service. A woman who has been absent from work because of pregnancy has the right to return to work up to 29 weeks after giving birth, but to qualify it is necessary for the woman to have had two years' continuous service at 11 weeks before the expected week of childbirth (see also p. 37). Women are entitled to Statutory Maternity Pay if they have worked for at least six months for the same employer before the expected time of giving birth.

- **DO I HAVE A RIGHT TO EQUAL OPPORTUNITIES AT WORK?** Equal opportunities mean that people should have the same employment opportunities, regardless of their sex, colour, race, nationality or ethnic origin. However, there are some situations where a person's sex or race is a vital part of the job qualification – a genuine occupational qualification. For example, certain kinds of employment like modelling, dramatic performance or personal social services may need to be carried out by a person of a particular sex or ethnic group.

- **DO I HAVE A RIGHT TO EQUAL PAY?** People who are employed on work which is rated as equivalent, of the same or broadly similar nature, or of equal value to that done by a member of the opposite sex are entitled to have the same pay and other terms and conditions of employment.

- **WHAT ABOUT EMPLOYING DISABLED PEOPLE?** Legislation introduced in 1995 includes a new right of non-discrimination in employment which will replace the quota provisions of the Disabled Persons (Employment) Act 1944. Under the new right, it will be unlawful for an employer with 20 or more staff to treat a disabled person less favourably than other people, unless there are justified reasons for doing so. Employers will also be required to consider reasonable adjustments to the terms on which they offer employment where this would overcome the practical effect of an individual's disability.

- **STATUTORY SICK PAY** Employers have a duty to pay Statutory Sick Pay (SSP) to employees who qualify under Department of Social Security rules. This is a minimum level of sick pay to most employees, aged between 16 and 65, who have been sick for four or more days in a row. Employees who are not eligible for SSP can claim Incapacity Benefit (which replaced sickness benefit in April 1995). Employers may claim compensation for SSP in certain circumstances.

FURTHER INFORMATION

Further information on employment rights can be found in the booklet Individual rights of employees, published by the **Department for Education and Employment** (PL 716). Guidance on the statutory scheme of maternity rights is available in the booklet Maternity rights (PL 958), published jointly by the **Department for Education and Employment** and the **Department of Social Security.**

Employment service

Unemployment and other benefits • Jobcentres • Job interviews •
Seminars and workshops • Jobclubs and work trials • Voluntary work •
Disability • Training

- **I'M UNEMPLOYED. WHAT SHALL I DO?** On the first day you are out of work contact your local jobcentre to see a New Client Adviser. You should also sign on for Unemployment Benefit immediately to avoid losing money through any delay. Unemployment Benefit provides payment for people who have lost their jobs. It is normally paid every two weeks for up to a year. If you cannot get Unemployment Benefit, you should apply for Income Support. You may also be able to get benefits if you are long-term sick or disabled, Housing Benefit to help you pay your rent, and Council Tax Benefit (see p. 57).

- **HOW CAN THE JOBCENTRE HELP ME?** If you are unemployed or expecting to lose your job soon, your local jobcentre is the best place to start looking for work. Your nearest jobcentre will be listed in the telephone book under Employment Services or Jobcentres. At jobcentres, job vacancies are displayed on cards. Staff there will give you more information about the jobs you are interested in. They will also be able to advise you about other job leads, such as newspaper advertisements and private employment agencies.

- **HOW CAN I GET MORE ADVICE?** At your local jobcentre, you can ask to see a Client Adviser, who can give extra help in finding a job. This includes helping you make a Back to Work plan. Your adviser can also give you information about In-Work Benefits.

- **CAN I GET HELP WITH INTERVIEW EXPENSES?** If you have to travel a long way for a job interview, you may be able to get financial help under the Travel to Interview scheme. The scheme helps with travel costs and overnight stay if the job you are applying for is full-time and permanent. The scheme is only available for people who have been out of work for more than four weeks.

- **WHAT IF I STILL CAN'T FIND A JOB?** If you are not back to work after three months, an adviser at the jobcentre will help you look again for vacancies and review your Back to Work plan. The adviser may also book a place for you at a job search seminar and a job review workshop. The seminars provide advice on interview technique and provide resources such as telephones and photocopiers to help you in applying for work. The workshops are designed to help you look at different career options.

- **WHAT IF I CAN'T FIND A JOB AFTER SIX MONTHS?** You will be offered another interview with your Client Adviser to update your Back to Work plan. The adviser may also offer other ways of getting back into work. These include a place on the Restart course, a place in a Jobclub, and Job Interview Guarantee. The Restart course helps you to think about how to make the best use of your skills, and to decide which jobs or training are best for you. Jobclubs are aimed at providing you with support and encouragement in your search for a job. They also provide telephone and other facilities free of charge. Job Interview Guarantee helps to match you with an employer who may give you a three-week work trial to see if you are suited for a particular vacancy.

- **WHAT IF I'VE BEEN OUT OF WORK FOR 12 MONTHS?** The jobcentre will offer you Jobplan Workshops and the opportunity to get involved in Community Action. The Jobplan Workshop lasts for five days and focuses on new options, and includes using a computer to match your skills to possible jobs or careers. Community Action gives you the chance to help local voluntary organisations and get some work experience.

- **WHAT IF I'M DISABLED AND UNEMPLOYED?** You can get advice and help from the jobcentre. Ask to be put in touch with the Disability Employment Adviser from your local Placing, Assessment and Counselling Team (see p. 99). The adviser can give advice on the sort of job that would suit you and put you in touch with suitable employers. The adviser can also give advice on getting equipment to help in your job, and arranging for you to register as disabled, if you are eligible.

• **WHAT TRAINING CAN I GET?** Training is provided through the Training and Enterprise Councils (TECs) in England and Wales. You can get information about them through your local jobcentre. TECs offer advice about training for a new job and learning new skills. Training courses include help with basic skills in reading, writing and numeracy. Young people (16–17 years of age) are guaranteed the offer of a suitable place on Youth Training with local employers, further education colleges, local authorities or voluntary organisations. People who have been out of work for at least six months are offered Training for Work, which may be in the form of job-specific training or work towards a National Vocational Qualification.

TECs also offer Open Learning, which is a self-access course using videos and computers. If you have been out of work for at least three months and want to go on a training course, TECs may be able to offer you a career development loan to cover the cost of fees and living expenses.

Redundancy

Consultation • Redundancy payment • Time off • Dismissal •
Industrial tribunals • Compensation • Further information

- **WHAT IS REDUNDANCY?** Redundancy occurs when your employer dismisses you because you are no longer needed at work, or because your employer's business has closed down.

- **CONSULTATION** Where a trade union represents employees, employers planning to make staff redundant must consult the union as soon as possible. The consultation must include talks on how to avoid or reduce the dismissals, and how to ease their effect. Consultation must take place even if the employees concerned do not belong to a union. Employers must try to reach agreement with the union, and should not give notice of dismissal until there has been full consultation.

- **WHO QUALIFIES FOR REDUNDANCY PAYMENT?** If you are an employee (full-time or part-time) who is made redundant, then your employer must make a payment to you provided you have completed two years' continuous service. You may also be entitled to redundancy payment if you leave a job because of your employer's behaviour. For example, if your employer does not keep to the basic terms of your contract, you can end the contract. This is called 'constructive dismissal'.

If you are laid off, or put on short-time, for at least four consecutive weeks, you may claim a redundancy payment. If you volunteer to leave your job you qualify for redundancy payment, provided your employer actually dismisses you.

In some cases, you may not qualify for a payment – for example, if you are on a fixed-term contract for less than two years, and if you agree in the contract not to claim redundancy payment.

- **HOW MUCH REDUNDANCY PAYMENT CAN I GET?** The size of a redundancy payment depends on three things:
- how long you have worked for your employer;
- your age; and
- your rate of pay.

One and a half weeks' pay is allowed for each complete year of employment between the ages of 41 and 64; one week's pay for each year of employment between the ages of 22 and 40; and half a week's pay for each year of employment between the ages of 18 and 21.

- **TIME OFF TO LOOK FOR WORK** If you have been working for an employer for at least two years and are given notice of redundancy, you have a right to reasonable time off during working hours to look for another job or arrange for training.

- **WHAT IS DISMISSAL?** There are a number of reasons why your employer might dismiss you. Redundancy has already been explained. You might also be dismissed for bad behaviour, illness or for not having the qualifications for the job. Whatever the situation, your employer must have a valid reason for dismissing you, and behave reasonably in dismissing you. Pressure on your employer, such as the threat of a strike, is not acceptable as a reason for dismissal.

- **WHAT CAN I DO ABOUT UNFAIR DISMISSAL?** You can make a complaint of general unfair dismissal to an industrial tribunal, provided you have worked for your employer (either full- or part-time) for at least two years. You can complain of unfair dismissal, regardless of hours or length of service, if the reason is:
- trade union membership or activities, or non-membership of a union;
- claiming a right under employment laws;
- maternity-related;
- taking certain action on health and safety grounds; or

- discrimination because of your sex or race.

You must normally make your complaint of unfair dismissal to an industrial tribunal within three months of the end of your job. Before the hearing there is an opportunity to settle the case through a conciliation officer. If that fails, then the case goes to the tribunal.

If the tribunal decides you have been unfairly dismissed, it will – after taking into account your wishes and what is practicable – order your employer to:

- reinstate you in your old job;
- re-engage you in a different job; or
- pay you compensation.

- **COMPENSATION FOR UNFAIR DISMISSAL** Normally, the tribunal makes a basic award and a compensatory award. The basic award is worked out in the same way as a redundancy payment (see p. 74). The amount of the compensatory award is decided by the tribunal according to the circumstances of each case, and takes into account, among other things, current and future loss of earnings and pension loss. The current maximum compensatory award is £11,000.

• FURTHER INFORMATION

For further information on redundancy and dismissal, these **Department for Education and Employment** *booklets are helpful:* Rights to Notice and Reasons for Dismissal (PL707);

Unfairly Dismissed? (PL712); Fair and Unfair Dismissal (PL714); Redundancy Payments (PL808); *and* Redundancy Consultation and Notification (PL833).

Setting up a business/ self-employment

Advice and training • Planning a business • Setting up a business • Finance • Business and the law • Self-employed or an employee? • Further information

- **ADVICE AND TRAINING** Starting and running your own business can be challenging and rewarding – and risky. Information and advice are available from a number of sources to help you make a success of things. Your first call should be to your local Training and Enterprise Council (TEC). In England, Business Links – advice centres bringing together in a single point of access all business support services (including TECs) in the area – offer a wide range of advisory services, including Business Planning and Business Training courses, which are offered free or at reduced rates. To find out where your nearest TEC or Business Link is situated, ask at your local jobcentre or look in the phone book. It may also be helpful to talk to your bank manager, as well as an accountant and a solicitor.

- **PLANNING A BUSINESS** To start in business, you need a product or service you can market and sell to potential customers. You need to know why customers should want to buy what you are offering, rather than what is already available. It is therefore important to be clear about the specific qualities of your product that make it better than rival products. You need to research the number and location of potential customers for your product, and how you should price and distribute it.

You will need to plan ahead by making an estimate of the amount of money needed to start up and run the business for an initial period of at least 12 months. This will take into account estimated income from the business balanced against expenditure on items such as buying or leasing a premises and capital equipment, employee costs, your salary, profession-al fees, expenses and repayment of any loans.

When you are ready to start, advertising and publicity in newspapers and magazines, and on television and radio, can be effective ways of getting customers.

- **SETTING UP A BUSINESS** There are a number of different ways of setting up in business. You can operate as a sole trader, with personal liability for all your business debts. You can go into a business partnership with other people, where you jointly share responsibility for debts. It is also possible to set up a limited company, run by one or more directors, with funds contributed in part or whole by shareholders who have a limited liability for the company's debts.

You may want to market your own product or service. Or you could buy an existing business, or set up a franchise business for an existing product. But before starting, it is important to decide whether you have the personal qualities – such as initiative, judgment and determination – necessary for survival in the competitive world of business.

- **FINANCE** Unless your start-up costs are low, launching a business usually requires financial investment. You may have your own funds which you can put into the business, or you may need to borrow money from a bank. Grants may be available from your local authority, the government or the European Union. Check whether your local TEC provides any financial support for business start-up.

- **BUSINESS AND THE LAW** If you are running a business, there are a number of laws you must comply with.

For tax assessment, you need to inform the Inland Revenue of your annual income and expenditure, and pay the required amount of tax. If you employ staff, you must deduct part of their pay as tax under the Pay-As-You-Earn (PAYE) system (see p. 152).

If your total sales income, or turnover, reaches a certain level, you must inform the local Value Added Tax (VAT) office of the Board of Customs and Excise that you need to register for VAT. After registering, you must charge VAT on all sales (apart from exempt or zero-rated goods) and pay VAT every quarter.

You must also pay National Insurance (NI, see p. 56) – covering contributory benefits such as Incapacity Benefit and retirement pensions – for yourself and make NI deductions for any employees, with some exceptions. You may also be responsible for paying Statutory Sick Pay and Statutory Maternity Pay to your employees. For information, contact your local social security office, or ring the Social Security Advice Line for Employers (free) on 0800 393539.

You are responsible for insurance at work, and the health and safety of any employees. For information, contact your local Health and Safety Executive office. If you are an employer, you have a number of legal duties concerning the rights of your staff. Contact your local jobcentre for information about subjects such as conditions of employment, redundancy, unfair dismissal, discrimination and trade union rights.

- **SELF-EMPLOYED OR AN EMPLOYEE?** An employed person pays tax and NI through the PAYE system. If you are self-employed, customers pay for the product or service you provide. It is your responsibility to submit your accounts to the Inland Revenue for tax and NI assessment. But there are some situations in which the Inland Revenue might classify you as employed, even though you think you are self-employed. For more information, contact your local tax office or jobcentre.

You may be both self-employed and work as an employee for another business. If so, you will probably have to pay tax and NI contributions for both kinds of work.

FURTHER INFORMATION

For further general information, see Starting and Running your own Business, by Dennis F. Millar, available from **Enterprise Publications (Cambridge) Limited** (Tel. 019542 61040). The following publications are available from the **Department of Trade and Industry**

(Tel. 0171 510 0169): Setting up in Business, Employing Staff; and A Guide to Help for Small Firms. For information on NI contributions, see Self-employed? (FB30), published by the **Benefits Agency.**

Safety at work

The scope of legislation • Regulatory bodies • What the law requires •
When to contact the Health and Safety Executive • Local authority
environmental officers • Further information

Health and safety in the workplace is covered by a range of laws and
regulations that apply throughout industry and business. A fundamental
principle of the health and safety system is that those who create risk from
work activity are responsible for the protection of workers and the public
from any consequences. However, employees are required to co-operate
with their employers in taking care.

On a day-to-day basis it is the employer's responsibility to decide which
regulations apply to their workforce and to implement them appropriate-
ly. To do this, information needs to be collected about the workplace – for
example, the jobs that employees do, what if any machinery is used,
whether there are several sites or establishments involved – and any hazards identified.

● **THE SCOPE OF LEGISLATION** The cornerstone of Britain's health
and safety legislation is the Health and Safety at Work etc. Act 1974, which
replaced and in some cases modernised previous health and safety regulations in England, Scotland and Wales.

As the Act covers many different types of working environments, it cannot
be specific in every detail. Some of the legal duties imposed by the Act are
mandatory, but the legislation also depends on both employers and
employees exercising a degree of personal responsibility for their own
health and safety. Some duties in the Act are expressed as goals or targets.
These need to be identified by everyone in the workplace and achieved 'in
so far as is reasonably practicable' or by exercising 'adequate control'. The

leaflet *HSW etc. Act, the Act outlined* is available free from the Health and Safety Executive (see below).

General fire precautions at most places of work are dealt with under the 1971 Fire Precautions Act by the fire authorities and the Home Office departments.

Six new sets of health and safety regulations came into force in 1993, in order to implement European Community directives. The new measures make some of what is already in the law more explicit. They also tackle new areas of health and safety at work – for example, display-screen equipment such as computer terminals.

- **GOVERNMENT BODIES** Regulatory bodies help administer, enforce and supervise the legislation and negotiate the implementation of EC directives in health and safety at work.

The Health and Safety Commission (HSC) has a number of functions, which include ensuring that established legislative standards in health and safety are maintained or improved.

The Health and Safety Executive (HSE) is the operating arm of the Commission. It has more direct contact with the public, and advises employers and employees on most safety matters on a day-to-day practical basis. It is the role of the HSE to:

- inspect some workplaces (but not all);
- investigate accidents and cases of ill health;
- enforce good standards, usually by advising people how to comply with the law, but sometimes by ordering them to make improvements and, if necessary, by prosecuting them;
- publish guidance and advice;
- provide an information service; and
- carry out research.

For information and advice you can contact your nearest HSE area office or the public enquiry centre in Sheffield (see Further information on p. 82). All enquiries are treated in the strictest confidence. If an inspector does investigate or visit your workplace, he or she will not identify the complainant without his or her consent.

- **WHAT THE LAW REQUIRES** The Health and Safety at Work etc. Act 1974 requires employers with five or more staff to prepare a written statement, specific to the company or organisation, setting out the general policy for protecting the health and safety of employees at work. The statement must also include arrangements for putting that policy into effective practice. The statement should be brought to the notice of all employees and revised whenever appropriate. Employers and employees should consult together in drawing up the statement which could say, for example:

- who should be alerted to, and make safe, potential hazards;

- who accidents should be reported to;

- who is responsible for safety inspections of machinery; and

- who should deal with fire, first aid and other emergencies. Arrangements for training those responsible should be made by the employer. The HSE produce a free guidance leaflet for employers on drafting a policy statement – *Writing a safety policy statement: Advice to employers*. Some trade associations and employers' associations have also produced guidance.

- **WHEN TO CONTACT THE HSE** If you believe your employer is exposing you to risks or not carrying out his or her legal duties, and if you have pointed this out without getting a satisfactory response, you can contact the HSE. If, as an employer, you are unsure how to comply with the law or make adequate health and safety provisions in your workplace, the HSE will advise you how to do this. The HSE may possibly send an inspector to make an assessment of your premises. If you are worried that your work might be affecting your health, the Employment Medical Advisory Service at the HSE will help and advise you accordingly.

If, as a member of the public, you think you have been harmed by a work activity, or have noticed something dangerous, you should also contact the HSE.

The HSE aims to answer simple telephone requests immediately but you will need to have all the necessary information at hand when you call. More complicated written requests usually take about ten days to deal with.

- **LOCAL AUTHORITY ENVIRONMENTAL OFFICERS** These officers monitor health and safety in shops, some warehouses, most offices, and places used for leisure and consumer services, hotels, restaurants and churches. You can contact them through the environmental health department of your local authority, or through your nearest Citizens Advice Bureau, which you will find listed in your local phone directory.

FURTHER INFORMATION

The **HSC** and **HSE** produce a range of leaflets and booklets on health and safety issues. The **HSE** has a public enquiry centre at Broad Lane, Sheffield S3 7HQ (Tel. 0114 2892000). The **HSC** can also be contacted at this address.

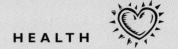

National Health Service •

Other forms of health care •

First aid training •

Disablement •

National Health Service

Services and organisation • Hospitals • The family doctor service •
Dentistry • Eye testing • Nursing care, preventive care and health education •
Complaints • Further information

What services are provided by the National Health Service?

The NHS offers a full range of medical and allied services provided by hospitals, general practitioners (GPs), dentists, pharmacists, opticians, district nurses and health visitors. These services are available to all people in Britain, regardless of income. Some forms of treatment, such as hospital care, are provided free, for others, there may be a charge.

How is the NHS funded?

Ninety six per cent of NHS funding comes from direct taxation – either through income tax or National Insurance contributions. The rest comes from payments made by patients towards the costs of certain services.

Who directs the NHS and how is it organised?

The Secretary of State for Health in England and the Secretary of State for Wales are responsible to Parliament for all aspects of the health services in their respective territories. At present a combination of regional, district and family health services authorities administer the NHS.

The eight regional health authorities (RHAs) are peculiar to England. Each plans the health services necessary for its particular region, involving resource allocation, major building projects and some specialised hospital services. They also provide funds for district health authorities (DHAs), family health services authorities (FHSAs), and fundholding GPs (see p. 86).[1]

[1] From April 1996 the RHAs will be replaced by eight regional offices of the NHS Executive, which develops and implements policies within the Department of Health; and the DHAs and FHSAs will be replaced by single all-purpose authorities.

At a more local level, DHAs are responsible for making sure there are adequate hospital and community health services in their areas. FHSAs manage the family doctor services provided by GPs and organise the local dentists, pharmacists and opticians.

Can local people influence how their services are managed?
Community health councils – one for each health district – reflect the views of local authorities, voluntary organisations and regional health authorities; meetings are open to the public. NHS Trusts are required to hold public meetings annually.

What kind of hospital services are available under the NHS?
District general hospitals provide a full range of treatment and diagnostic services for in-patients, day-patients and out-patients, as well as maternity departments, infectious disease units, rehabilitation services, and psychiatric and geriatric facilities. There are specialist hospitals or units for children, for the mentally ill, the elderly and for the treatment of specific diseases. Teaching hospitals combine treatment facilities with training medical students.

Who runs these hospitals?
Nearly all NHS hospital and community health services are now managed as NHS Trusts. These are self-governing units, run by boards of directors, with the freedom to set staff numbers and pay rates. Their income comes mainly from NHS contracts to provide services to health authorities and GP fundholders.

If I need hospital treatment, will I have long to wait?
The Government has made cutting hospital waiting lists a priority; under the Patient's Charter, every patient can expect to be admitted to hospital within 18 months of being placed on a waiting list. You should have to wait no longer than 26 weeks for a first out-patient appointment when referred to hospital by your GP.

What is the family doctor service?
This is the service provided by GPs, either working singly, in partnerships or group practices. In England and Wales it is organised in each area by the family health services authorities. GPs are paid according to the number of patients they have.

GPs are funded by their family health services authorities. Practices with more than 7,000 patients (5,000 from April 1996) may apply to become GP fundholders, becoming responsible for their own NHS budget, which they use to buy the best value services for their patients. Smaller practices may group together to meet the size requirement.

How do I find a GP?

Everyone has the right to register with a GP, and people over 16 can choose their own doctor. Doctors can accept or refuse to take a person as their patient. Patients need not necessarily find their own GP. Under the Patient's Charter, your family health services authority should provide you with information about how to change your GP, and a list of GPs in the area, within two working days of your request. Additionally, your family health services authority should find you a GP within two working days of a request.

If you are away from home and need a doctor, you can get treatment from a local GP if you ask to be treated as a temporary resident.

What sort of treatment can my GP provide?

Your GP can provide diagnosis and treatment of everyday illnesses, including prescribing necessary drugs, and can refer you to specialist services when necessary. Most treatment from your GP is free. Your doctor will treat you in the surgery or, if necessary, will visit you at home. Many doctors' surgeries are now situated in health centres, where there is a team of medical workers including district nurses, health visitors and midwives.

If you need hospital treatment, your GP will discuss it with you and refer you to the hospital best suited to your needs. If your doctor is a fundholding GP, this may be a hospital in the public or private sector. Non-fundholding GPs send patients to the hospital with which the district health authority has a contract.

Do I have to pay for medicines prescribed by my NHS doctor?

There is a charge for each item on the prescription, with the exception of contraceptives. However, prescription charges do not apply to the following people:

- children under 16 years (or young people under 19 and still in full-time education);

- expectant mothers and women who have had a baby in the past year;
- women aged 60 and over and men aged 65 and over;
- patients suffering from certain specified medical conditions;
- war and armed forces disablement pensioners (for prescriptions which relate to the disability for which they receive a war pension); and
- people in families in receipt of Income Support, Family Credit or Disability Working Allowance.

A declaration on the back of the prescription form has to be completed by those exempt from payment. If you do not qualify for exemption, you can buy a prescription 'season ticket', lasting for four months or a year.

Will my local chemist dispense medicines under the NHS?

Most pharmacy owners in Britain have arrangements with their local family health services authority to dispense medicines under the NHS. They display a notice to this effect in their pharmacies.

How do I get dental care under the NHS?

Family health services authorities are responsible for organising local dental services for their particular areas.

To receive dental care under the NHS you have to register with a dentist for 'continuing care and treatment' for two years. This provides for the full range of dental treatment; your dentist must also give you an information leaflet about his practice, and a treatment plan showing details of costs.

If you need a dentist when you are away from home you can sign on as an occasional patient with a local dentist. This provides for emergency treatment, but does not entitle you to the full range of treatments.

What do I have to pay for?

There are proportional charges for most types of NHS dental treatment, including examinations. You have to pay for 80 per cent of the cost of your treatment up to an agreed maximum. The following people are specifically exempt from dental charges:

- all those under 18 (or 19 if in full-time education);
- women who were pregnant when the dentist accepted them for treatment or who have had a baby in the past year;

- people in families receiving Income Support or Family Credit; and
- people in families assessed as having a low income.

What about sight tests?
Sight tests are free to:

- children;
- people in families receiving Income Support, Family Credit or Disability Working Allowance;
- people in families assessed as having a low income; and
- those with specified medical needs.

Children, people on low incomes, and those requiring certain complex lenses receive a voucher towards the cost of their spectacles.

Nursing care, preventive care and health education
If you need help after coming home from hospital you may receive visits from a district nurse. During pregnancy and childbirth your GP will take care of you, assisted by a midwife, who will share in your antenatal and post-natal care. Your health visitor and local child-health clinic will advise you on, for example, your children's development and vaccination requirements.

What if I have a complaint about NHS services?
Complaints about a hospital or community health service can be made to the person who provided the service or to their complaints officer. If you want to complain about your GP, dentist, optician or pharmacist, you may be able to use the practice's own complaints procedure. If not, you can complain to your family health services authority. Your local community health council can provide advice and information on how to complain. If you are not satisfied with the response, you may approach the Health Service Commissioner (Ombudsman), who investigates complaints from members of the public about health service bodies (excluding complaints about clinical judgments, family practitioners, personnel matters and the use of a health authority's discretionary powers.

FURTHER INFORMATION

The addresses of your local district health authority, family health services authority and community health council will be in your phone book.

The **Office of the Health Service Commissioner** is at Church House, Great Smith Street, London SW1P 3BW.

Other forms of health care

Private health care • Private dental care •

Complementary medicine/therapies • Further information

How can the 'average person' afford private health care?

Joining an insurance scheme provides for private health care in return for an annual subscription. Some schemes have an upper age limit (for example 75). The Government has introduced tax relief on private health insurance premiums paid by people over 60, to encourage people in this age group to join.

BUPA (British United Provident Association) is the largest private health care organisation in Britain, currently covering over 3 million people.

What do private health care schemes cover?

In general these schemes cover medical and hospital bills. There are, however, different schemes to suit individual circumstances. For example, some schemes allow people to choose to receive treatment only in the local private hospital, or to exclude out-patient consultation. General exclusions from cover include maternity care, seeing a GP privately, and cosmetic treatments.

Many schemes cover all members of the family. There are also group schemes which can be arranged by companies for their employees, as part of the salary package.

What are the advantages of private health care?

There are no differences in the quality of medical treatment provided by the private sector and the NHS. However, private health care guarantees a private room in hospital and generally more luxurious surroundings. Also, the waiting time to see a consultant or to start treatment will generally be cut by going privately.

So is it a straight choice between private health care and the NHS?

Not necessarily. The Government is anxious to encourage co-operation between the private sector and the NHS, and NHS patients are sometimes treated in the private sector to reduce waiting lists. There are also pay-beds in some NHS hospitals, and expensive facilities and equipment are often shared.

What about dental care?

There are also insurance schemes providing private dental care. They provide for regular check-ups with a dentist belonging to the particular scheme, routine dental work such as fillings, and emergency dental treatment.

Cosmetic treatment may be excluded, as well as orthodontic appliance therapy; if you need treatment involving a dental laboratory, such as crowns or bridges, you may have to pay for the laboratory costs.

What is complementary medicine or complementary therapy?

Complementary medicine can cover a range of therapies and practices, the best known forms of which are probably osteopathy, chiropractic, homoeopathy and acupuncture. Lesser known ones include reflexology, hypnotherapy, iridology, radionics and crystal therapy.

What if I want to consider having some kind of complementary therapy?

Complementary therapy, with the exception perhaps of homoeopathy, is usually only available outside the NHS, and as it is not commonly included in private health insurance schemes, you will almost certainly have to pay for such treatment yourself. It would be sensible to have a word with your GP before deciding on a course of complementary treatment. This is particularly important if you are already having NHS treatment of some kind, or have developed some health problem which you have not yet discussed with him or her. The following paragraphs give a little more information about the common kinds of complementary therapy.

What is acupuncture?

Acupuncture is traditionally a branch of Chinese medicine which involves inserting needles in particular parts of the body; the needles may be manipulated or may have a small electric current passed through them. Acupuncture is sometimes used for pain relief; practitioners believe it to be effective in treating a variety of other disorders including asthma, migraine and osteoarthritis, and to induce anaesthesia. Some 'conventional' doctors have also studied acupuncture techniques, but most acupuncturists are not medically qualified.

The British Medical Acupuncture Society has a list of practising members who are also qualified doctors, to whom you may be referred by your own GP (see Further information).

What is osteopathy?
Osteopathy is a system of diagnosis and treatment whose main emphasis is on conditions affecting the spine and joints. It uses gentle manual and manipulative methods of treatment.

Osteopathy is the first complementary therapy to have achieved state regulation. The General Osteopathic Council is responsible for developing, promoting and regulating the profession. To find a qualified osteopath contact one of the osteopathic organisations listed at the end of this section.

What is chiropractic?
Chiropractic is similar to osteopathy, but uses different manipulative movements and includes use of spinal X-rays for diagnosis of mechanical problems. The General Chiropractic Council (which is expected to have been set up by early 1996) will be responsible for ensuring the profession is properly regulated. The chiropractic organisation given at the end of this section can be contacted for advice about finding a chiropractor practising in your area.

What is homoeopathy?
The principle behind homoeopathic medicine is that 'like cures like' – that is, tiny quantities, greatly diluted, are given of substances which in larger amounts are known to produce the symptoms to be cured. Homoeopathic remedies are most commonly prescribed for allergies, stomach complaints and pain in joints; they are not usually used for life-threatening illnesses.

A homoeopathic doctor will look at the patient as a whole – lifestyle, personality, family history as well as the symptoms of the illness – when considering a remedy. Remedies are prepared from repeatedly diluted extracts of, for example, minerals and plants.

The British Homoeopathic Association has members who are qualified doctors as well as being qualified in homoeopathic medicine. The Society of Homoeopaths' members are qualified homoeopaths but are not qualified doctors.

Some GPs may prescribe homoeopathic medicines, and some may be willing to refer patients (either under the NHS or privately) to one of the very few NHS hospitals or units which specialise in providing treatment based on homoeopathic principles.

Some kinds of homoeopathic products can be bought without prescription from pharmacies.

If I consult a practitioner of complementary medicine, how can I be sure he or she is properly qualified?
You should consult the appropriate professional body (where one exists), which will have a list of registered practitioners with details of training and qualifications. As mentioned earlier, it is also advisable to seek advice from your GP before embarking on a course of complementary treatment.

FURTHER INFORMATION

Addresses

• **British Medical Acupuncture Society,** Newton House, Newton Lane, Lower Whitley, Warrington WA4 4JA (Tel. 01925 730727).

• **British Acupuncture Association and Register,** 34 Aldernay Street, London SW1V 4EU (Tel. 0171 834 1012).

• **British Homoeopathic Association,** 27a Devonshire Street, London W1N 1RJ (Tel. 0171 935 2163).

• **Society of Homoeopaths,** 2 Artizan Road, Northampton NN1 4HU (Tel. 01604 21400).

• **Faculty of Homoeopaths,** Royal London Homoeopathic Hospital, Great Ormond Street, London WC1N 3HR (Tel. 0171 837 8833).

• **General Council and Register of Osteopaths,** 56 London Street, Reading, Berkshire RG1 4SQ (Tel. 01734 576585).

• **British Osteopathic Association,** 8–10 Boston Place, London NW1 6QH (Tel. 0171 262 1128).

• **Natural Therapeutic and Osteopath Society and Register,** London School of Osteopathy, 8 Lanark Square, Glengall Bridge, London E14 9RE (Tel. 0171 538 8334).

• **College of Osteopaths,** 13 Furzehill Road, Borehamwood, Herts WD6 2DG (Tel. 0181 905 1395).

• **British Chiropractic Association,** 29 Whitley Street, Reading RG2 0EG (Tel. 01734 757557).

First aid training

Courses • Qualifications • First aid at work • Volunteers •
Further information

● **USE IN EMERGENCY** People who have received first aid training should be able to treat minor injuries themselves and, in an emergency, should know how to keep an injured person alive and to minimise the consequences of injury or illness until a doctor or nurse arrives.

Who provides such training?

Most first aid training in Britain is provided by the St John Ambulance (60 per cent) and the British Red Cross (20 per cent). Both organisations offer courses or demonstrations for specific groups – for instance, mother and toddler groups or youth group leaders. Some private companies are also involved in first aid training.

What topics are covered?

Topics include basic resuscitation, control of bleeding, treatment of unconsciousness, shock, treatment for minor injuries, burns, scalds, fractures and sprains, how to cope with poisoning, epilepsy, asthma, heart attacks and strokes. Courses include theoretical and practical work. Whether or not you have an examination depends on the course: some are examined, others provide a Certificate of Attendance.

How do I find out about courses?

Contact your local education authority or the county headquarters of St John Ambulance or the British Red Cross (numbers are listed in your local phone book); your local library may also be able to help. There is a nominal fee for courses that, in the case of St John Ambulance and the British Red Cross, goes towards financing their voluntary work. There is also a fee for adult education classes but many people, for example those who are unemployed or on Income Support, are entitled to concessionary rates.

What if I do not have time for a long course?

Ideally you should do a course to practise your skills; however, watching a video or consulting a book will go some way to equipping you with the knowledge. Both St John Ambulance and the British Red Cross sell a wide range of books and videos, and general first aid manuals can be found in libraries and bookshops. The British Red Cross and St John Ambulance also run two-hour courses which teach the very basics of first aid.

Are there any courses specifically for children?

St John Ambulance runs the Three Cross Award Scheme, which is used in schools with pupils from nine years of age onwards. It consists of a comprehensive, video-based package of support materials used by teachers to train their pupils in basic first aid. Pupils receive certificates as each stage of the scheme is successfully completed. First aid is also taught to St John Ambulance's junior members (from six years of age).

Does first aid training count towards any academic qualifications?

The General National Vocational Qualifications (GNVQs) in Health and Social Care and National Vocational Qualifications (NVQs) in Care, Child Care and Sports and Recreation contain an element on skills in coping in an emergency. First aid training can help you gain the necessary skills and knowledge.

What about first aid at work?

The Health and Safety Regulations of 1981 stipulate that employers must have a sufficient number of suitably qualified and trained people who can give first aid when required – about one in every 50 workers. Their training and qualification must be approved by the Health and Safety Executive.

Who provides first aid at work training?

St John Ambulance is the main provider of training to meet Health and Safety Regulations, followed by the British Red Cross. The highest level of training provided by St John Ambulance is the First Aid at Work course – a four-day intensive course which ends with an examination and is suitable for high risk occupations. The next level is the Appointed Persons course (one day), suitable for a low-risk working environment.

Is there any first aid training specific to particular occupations?
Bodies such as the police force and the fire brigade undergo prescribed training courses. For teachers and other school staff, St John Ambulance runs four- to six-hour courses which cover basic first aid for children.

Are there any occasions on which trained first aiders must be present?
Football stadiums and other sporting venues must have qualified first aiders at pre-set ratios. First aid cover at all kinds of public events is provided by St John Ambulance and the British Red Cross, and includes ambulances and mobile first aid units. All such first aid workers are volunteers.

What level of training do these volunteers receive?
Volunteers are trained according to each organisation's national pro-gramme. St John Ambulance's volunteers have to hold the First Aid at Work certificate and complete specific training not available to the general public; this training is regularly updated throughout the year. To become a first aid trainer, you must also undergo special training.

FURTHER INFORMATION

The headquarters of the **St John Ambulance** are at 1 Grosvenor Crescent, London SW1X 7EF and those of the **British Red Cross,** at 9 Grosvenor Crescent, London SW1X 7EJ. The local headquarters of these organisations are listed in your phone book. For more details about the **Heath and Safety Executive** see p. 80.

Disablement

What aids are available to help disabled people cope with everyday life?
There is a range of equipment designed to meet particular needs: hearing aids, low-vision aids, electronic communication aids, mechanical chairs to help people get up from a sitting position, aids for showering and bathing, and wheelchairs (non-powered and electrically-powered) for children and adults.

Much equipment is supplied free by the National Health Service or can be borrowed from the local authority; contact your GP or your social services department. Disabled living centres allow you to try out a whole range of special equipment. The Disabled Living Foundation provides advice on daily living equipment.

What about help in the home?
The Home Help Service, provided by local authorities, provides help with domestic and personal care, while the Meals on Wheels Service (see p. 118) delivers a hot midday meal to people who cannot cook for themselves. Through the Independent Living Fund, seriously disabled people can get financial help to pay for the support they need to continue living at home.

Disabled facilities grants, administered by local authorities and available to both property owners and tenants, help with essential house adaptations – for example, installing ramps for wheelchairs or putting in a downstairs shower or lavatory.

What if living at home becomes impossible?
There is some specially designed housing for disabled people who are able to look after themselves. Sheltered housing (groups of flats or bungalows complete with resident warden, who can provide immediate help if required) offers another solution. This type of accommodation is provided by local authorities, housing associations or private companies. Others may find life easier in residential accommodation, either on a long-term basis or after coming out of hospital.

What about transport?
In many areas, buses have been modified with lower steps and non-slip surfaces to make for easier access, and some London buses are specially designed to take wheelchairs. The main rail stations and airports all have facilities for disabled people and there are concessionary fare schemes on both buses and trains.

For disabled people who cannot manage public transport, local authorities and voluntary organisations provide transport to day centres, hospitals and workshops. There are also door-to-door schemes such as Dial-a-Ride. Specially adapted cars can be obtained through Motability (see p. 120), while the Orange Badge Scheme operates nationally to provide parking concessions for disabled people.

What about access to buildings?
All new public buildings must provide access for people with physical disabilities and take account of the needs of those with sensory impairments. Many older buildings are also being similarly modified.

What opportunities are there to take part in sport?
The British Sports Association for the Disabled co-ordinates sports for people with disabilities. It operates through local clubs and organises competitions, coaching and training.

What benefits are there for disabled people?
A new contributory Incapacity Benefit replaced sickness benefit and invalidity benefit from April 1995. The new benefit has three rates depending on the number of weeks of incapacity and also comprises certain age additions and increases for adult and child dependants.

Severe Disablement Allowance is a tax-free benefit for people between 16 and 65 years of age who have not been able to work for at least 28 weeks because of illness or disability but who cannot get Incapacity Benefit because they have not paid enough National Insurance contributions. Those over 20 years of age when they first became incapable of work must also be assessed as at least 80 per cent disabled.

Disability Living Allowance is a non-contributory, tax-free benefit for disabled adults and children who need help to look after themselves or to get about. It has a care component and a mobility component.

A non-contributory, tax-free Attendance Allowance may be payable to people severely disabled at or after age 65 who have personal care needs, depending on the amount of attention they require.

Disability Working Allowance is a non-contributory, tax-free benefit which tops up the earnings of people who work 16 hours or more a week, but whose earning capacity is limited because of their disability.

What if I become disabled as a result of my job or through service in the armed forces?

Industrial Injuries Disablement Benefit may be claimed by people who become disabled as a result of an accident at work or of a disease recognised as a risk in particular occupations (not applicable to the self-employed).

Anyone disabled as a result of service in the armed forces at any time since 1914 is entitled to claim a pension. The Department of Social Security deals with claims which relate to service between 1914 and September 1921 and from 3 September 1939 onwards; the Ministry of Defence deals with claims for the intervening period, from October 1921 to 2 September 1939.

Are there any benefits for carers?

Invalid Care Allowance is a taxable, non-contributory, non-means-tested benefit. The allowance is available to carers between 16 and pensionable age who have given up the opportunity of full-time paid employment to provide regular and substantial care (of at least 35 hours a week) to a severely disabled person receiving either the higher or middle rate of Disability Living Allowance care component or Attendance Allowance.

A carer premium is available for those who are entitled to Invalid Care Allowance and receiving at least one of the following benefits: Income Support, Housing Benefit or Council Tax Benefit.

What provision is made for educating children with disabilities?
Wherever possible, children with special needs (learning difficulties, physical or sensory impairment) are educated in ordinary schools with appropriate support units attached. There are also special schools for severely physically disabled children and those who are blind or deaf.

Local education authorities are required to assess and make provision for educating children with special needs, taking into account the views of the parents.

What about further/higher education?
Universities and colleges must explain in their prospectuses their provisions for disabled students. A disabled students' allowance, additional to the normal student grant, is available at the discretion of local education authorities.

What about employment?
All of the Employment Service's programmes (see p. 70) make provisions for people with disabilities. Services for people with disabilities are delivered through local integrated specialist teams – Placing, Assessment and Counselling Teams (PACTs). They are supported by regional Ability Development Centres, which carry out training and development work, and provide special advice for employers who may be considering employing people with disabilities. A range of programmes (for example, offering sheltered employment opportunities) is available for disabled people who need specialist help.

FURTHER INFORMATION

A useful source of information is the Disability Rights Handbook, *revised for each tax year and published by the* **Disability Alliance Educational and Research Association.**

Other contacts include:

- **British Sports Association for the Disabled,** The Mary Glen Haig Suite, Solecast House, 13–27 Brunswick Place, London N1 6DX (Tel. 0171 490 4919).
- **The Disabled Living Foundation,** 380 Harrow Road, London W9 2HU (Tel. 0171 289 6111).
- **The Royal Association for Disability and Rehabilitation (RADAR),** 12 City Forum, 250 City Road, London EC1V 8AF (Tel. 0171 250 3222).

- **The Royal National Institute for the Blind,** 224 Great Portland Street, London W1N 6AA (Tel. 0171 388 1266).
- **The Royal National Institute for Deaf People,** 105 Gower Street, London WC1E 6AH (Tel. 0171 387 8033).
- **Disability Wales,** Llys Ifor, Crescent Road, Caerphilly, Mid Glamorgan CF8 1XL (Tel. 01222 887325).
- **Carers' National Association,** Ruth Pitter House, 20–25 Glasshouse Yard, London EC1A 4JS (Tel. 0171 490 8818).

Nursery education •

Schooling •

Higher and further education •

Nursery education

Nursery education for children under five is not compulsory and a place for your child cannot be guaranteed. However, the Government has launched a voucher scheme to provide a pre-school place (phased in over time) for all four-year-olds whose parents wish to take it up. The first places will become available in a limited number of areas from April 1996. Although local government education authorities are free to provide nursery education for children, the scale of such provision varies markedly. To find out more about nursery educational provision in your area contact your own local education authority.

You may be able to send your child to a private nursery, which should be registered with the local authority. The authority must ensure that the person applying for registration and anyone looking after your child is fit and qualified to do so. Conditions can be imposed on the running of the nursery, for example specifying the number of children to be looked after and the number of staff required to do this job.

An alternative to state nursery-school provision is offered by playgroups, many of which are members of the Pre-School Learning Alliance. In England, for instance, nearly 800,000 children attend playgroups organised by the Alliance, which is a national educational charity. Most playgroups are organised by parents and meet in places like church, village and community halls. The Alliance organises training courses for parents, playgroup staff, volunteers, trainers and field workers. Registered playgroup workers may train for the Diploma in Playgroup Practice. If playgroups have children for more than two hours a day, the premises and anyone in charge of the children have to be registered with the local authority.

FURTHER INFORMATION

Details about the **Pre-School Learning** **Alliance's** *work is obtainable from its headquarters at 61–63 King's Cross Road, London WC1X 9LL*

(Tel. 0171 833 0991) or its regional offices, whose details may be found in the phone book.

Schooling

Choosing a school • School management • Inspections • Curriculum •
Special educational needs • Independent schools • Alternative provision •
Further information

Under the law you must ensure that your child receives full-time education between the ages of five and 16. About 93 per cent of school pupils receive free education in state schools, while others go to independent schools financed from fees paid by parents.

- **HOW DO I CHOOSE A SCHOOL FOR MY CHILD?** You have the right to express a preference for a particular state school for your child although this cannot always be met since the school may be full of children with a stronger claim. In order to help you choose, schools have to publish a prospectus providing information about examination and curriculum test results, admissions policy and attendance figures.

Priority may be given to children with brothers or sisters in the school or who live in a clearly defined catchment area. If your choice of school is not met, you have the right to appeal to an independent committee. Your child must be admitted to your choice of school if the committee rules in your favour.

What information should I receive?

Every year your school must give you a written annual report on the education of your child. This report has to contain a summary of your child's progress in school curriculum subjects, including the results of any assessment tests. Information is also provided on qualifications gained by your child. Reports also have to give details about your child's attendance record and general progress and information about the arrangements for discussing the report with teachers.

School governors must give you an annual report about the school, its finances and the date, time and place of the annual parents' meeting, where you can discuss the school report and raise with the school governors and the head teacher any concerns you may have about the running of the school.

- **HOW IS THE SCHOOL MANAGED?** All state schools have a governing body on which parents are represented. Parent governors are elected by parents of pupils registered at the school. Full details about the election system are obtainable from the school or your local education authority. The other governors consist of representatives from teachers at the school, business people and others working in the local community. Minutes recording the proceedings of governors' meetings are available at the school for you to see.

Can the school become self-governing?

If you live in England or Wales and your child attends a local authority-controlled school, you and other parents have the right to vote on whether that school should apply to be free of local authority control. If parents vote in favour of this, the school applies to the Government for grant-maintained status. If the application is approved the governing body becomes fully responsible for running the school (within the laws that apply to all state schools). This includes managing the whole budget and employing teachers and other staff. This type of school receives its funding from central government. In England, this is distributed by the Funding Agency for Schools.

- **IS THE SCHOOL SUBJECT TO INDEPENDENT INSPECTION?** In order to maintain standards, your school is inspected by independent inspectors every four or five years. Before the inspection takes place, you have the right to put your views about the school to the inspection team. A readable summary of the inspection report is sent to you and the full report is published. School governors must prepare an action plan to follow up the report and then come back to you by providing information about the progress made in carrying out the report's main recommendations. Full information about the inspection process is available from your local school, which will have copies of the most recent inspection reports.

• **WHAT SUBJECTS ARE TAUGHT IN SCHOOLS?** If your child is between the ages of five and 14, and attends a maintained school in England or Wales, he or she must be taught the core subjects of the National Curriculum – English, maths and science – together with the other foundation subjects, which are technology (design and technology, and information technology), history, geography, music, art and physical education. A modern foreign language is also compulsory from the age of 11. In Wales, Welsh is a core subject in Welsh-speaking schools.

There is greater flexibility for pupils aged 14 to 16. Art, music, history and geography cease to be compulsory, although most schools continue to offer these subjects. From September 1996, the National Curriculum minimum requirements for 14- to 16-year-olds will be English, maths, science, physical education, and a short course in both technology and a modern foreign language. Schools should typically be able to teach the National Curriculum requirements, and religious education, in 60 per cent of the teaching week for 14- to 16-year-olds, leaving them free to decide how best to use the remaining 40 per cent to meet the needs of their pupils.

Religious education is compulsory in all state schools, although you have the right to withdraw your child from these classes. State secondary schools are required to provide sex education for their pupils. Primary school governors decide whether or not to offer sex education to their pupils. You are entitled to withdraw your child from sex education classes other than those required by the National Curriculum Science Order.

Your child's progress is regularly assessed by teachers, and through national tests at 7, 11 and 14 for English and maths, and at 11 and 14 for science. Teacher assessment and test results are given equal status and are reported directly to you by the school. Sixteen-year-olds are assessed by the General Certificate of Secondary Education (GCSE) examination.

• **SPECIAL EDUCATIONAL NEEDS** If your child has special educational needs, comprising learning difficulties of all kinds, the local education authority is required to assess what these needs are and how best to cater for them. As the parent, you have the right to be involved in decisions about your child's special education. Wherever possible, children with special educational needs are educated in ordinary schools.

Placement in an ordinary school must be compatible with the needs of the child and with the provision of efficient education for the other children in the school.

- **INDEPENDENT SCHOOLS** Fee-paying independent schools must register with the appropriate education department and are open to inspection. Fees may vary from around £300 a term for day pupils at nursery age to over £4,000 a term for senior boarding pupils. Some schools offer bursaries to help pupils from less well-off families. Such pupils may also be helped by local education authorities or by the Government's Assisted Places Scheme (see Further information).

- **ALTERNATIVE PROVISION** There is no legal obligation on parents to educate their children at school, provided the local education authority is satisfied that the child is receiving a suitable course of study. Advice on educating children at home can be obtained from Education Otherwise (see below).

FURTHER INFORMATION

For general enquiries about schools in your area speak to your local education authority, which will be listed in your local phone book.

Addresses
- **Office for Standards in Education (OFSTED)**, 29–33 Kingsway, London WC2B 6SE (Tel. 0171 421 6800).
- **School Curriculum and Assessment Authority,** Newcombe House, 45 Notting Hill Gate, London W11 3JB (Tel. 0171 229 1234).

- **Independent Schools Information Service,** 56 Buckingham Gate, London SW1E 6AE (Tel. 0171 630 8793).
- **Assisted Places Committee,** 26 Queen Anne's Gate, London SW1H 9AN (Tel. 0171 222 9595).
- **Education Otherwise,** P.O. Box 7420, London N9 9SG (Tel. 0891 518303).

Higher and further education

- **HOW DO I GO ON TO HIGHER EDUCATION?** Schools and further education colleges in England and Wales offer General Certificate of Education Advanced (A) level and Advanced Supplementary (AS) courses and advanced General National Vocational Qualifications (GNVQs), which are the springboard for higher education courses in universities and elsewhere. Two or three A-level passes (grades A to C or equivalent) or one advanced GNVQ, sometimes with one GCE A-level or additional GNVQ units, are usually required to secure a university place. In recent years there has been an increase in the number of students being admitted to universities with so-called 'non-traditional' qualifications and some mature students are admitted to universities without formal qualifications.

- **HOW DO I APPLY?** For most undergraduate degree courses, DipHE (Diploma in Higher Education) and HND (Higher National Diploma) courses at universities and colleges, you should apply through the central agency – UCAS (the Universities and Colleges Admissions Service). For some art and design courses application should be made through the Art and Design Admissions Registry (ADAR). The UCAS application form offers you a maximum of eight university choices. Each institution provides prospective students with a prospectus setting out full details of all the courses and facilities offered. UCAS publishes a handbook listing all the institutions in the UCAS scheme and the courses which they expect to offer.

You must complete your application form and send it to UCAS between 1 September and 15 December for courses beginning in October of the following year. If you wish to go to Oxford or Cambridge University, you must also apply directly to these universities (by 15 October in the year before entry). Once the forms are received by UCAS, copies are sent to the institutions you have chosen on your form. They in turn make their decisions on your applications and UCAS informs you of the results. Universities usually make you a conditional offer of acceptance which requires you to obtain specific grades in GCE A-level or other examinations, such as GNVQs. If you fulfil the conditions you are then offered the place. UCAS organises a clearing scheme in late August and September to match remaining vacancies with unplaced applicants.

In addition to the UCAS handbook, you can use the services of ECCTIS – a computerised, government-supported information service – which has over 80,000 course records on its database in over 700 universities and colleges in Britain. It also includes the contents of the UCAS handbook.

Courses and Degrees
Higher education courses consist of first degrees (mainly full-time lasting three or more years), postgraduate degrees and courses leading to professional qualifications. Postgraduate courses usually involve advanced research work. An undergraduate course generally has to be successfully completed before work can start on a postgraduate degree. If you wish to go on a postgraduate course, you have to apply directly to the institution concerned.

- **CAN I GET ANY FINANCIAL ASSISTANCE?** If you are on a higher education first degree or comparable designated course, financial assistance is available in the form of awards and loans. Awards are paid from public funds and consist of a means-tested grant which helps pay living costs and a payment which meets the costs of tuition. Your parents are expected to contribute towards the grant if their income is above a certain level. Awards are payable by your local education authority in England and Wales.

Your grant can be topped up by a loan obtainable from the Student Loans Company Ltd. Loans are not means tested. Your loan has to be paid back to the company in monthly instalments after you complete your course. Students should apply for a loan through their university or college.

If you are in serious financial difficulties, you may receive selective discretionary help from limited access funds kept by universities or colleges.

You can also be sponsored by an employer; under this arrangement you work for the employer for about three or four months in the year and the employer supplements your grant. Information about sponsorship is available from the Careers and Occupational Information Centre (Tel. 0114 2594563). Employers sponsor courses in engineering, specialised science subjects, business studies and related subjects.

The European Union provides top-up grants if you wish to study in another member state. Grants are also payable to meet the costs of foreign language study in another member state. Your university or college will give you full information about the programmes under which the grants are available.

- **OPEN UNIVERSITY** The Open University is a non-residential university offering degree and other courses for adult students of all ages. Formal academic qualifications are not required to register for most courses, but the standards of the University's degrees are the same as those of other universities. The academic year begins in February and applications have to be sent in by the previous September. Three-quarters of Open University students have jobs and study on a part-time basis.

- **FURTHER EDUCATION** Many students choose to take vocational courses in further education colleges which also provide GCE A-level courses. Vocational courses lead to nationally recognised qualifications, and may cover information technology, computing, business studies, foreign languages, engineering, construction and office administration. There are strong ties with industry and commerce.

If you want to continue your education at a further education college, you should apply directly to your local college, which will provide you with a prospectus outlining the courses and facilities offered and the entry requirements. Fees are not charged by colleges if you are between the ages of 16 and 18 and are studying a full-time course. If you are studying part-time, you may have to pay fees; this also applies if you are on a full- or part-time course and you are aged 19 or over. You can get tax relief if you are paying fees for certain courses. Your college will advise you on this. Your local education authority has the power to make discretionary awards to students on further education courses.

Qualifications

The General National Vocational Qualification (GNVQ) is an alternative to traditional GCE A-level and AS-level courses. GNVQs provide a broad-based education which enables you to acquire basic vocational skills and knowledge. GNVQ courses are available at three levels: Foundation, Intermediate and Advanced (the Advanced GNVQ being broadly equivalent to two GCE A-levels). They are offered in colleges by the Business and Technology Education Council, City and Guilds of London Institute and the RSA Examinations Board. Awarding bodies work in partnership with colleges and business.

Job-specific National Vocational Qualifications (NVQs) are based on standards developed by industry and commerce. They test your ability to do a job and are assessed in workplace conditions. The National Council for Vocational Qualifications decides whether qualifications follow NVQ criteria. If they do, the Council approves the award.

Further education for adults

The Further Education Funding Councils (FEFCs) for England and Wales and local education authorities are together responsible for securing the provision of all types of further education for adults. The FEFCs work through further education colleges to provide courses which lead to academic or vocational qualifications; basic skills courses; courses to develop proficiency in English as a second language; and courses for students with learning difficulties. Local education authorities are responsible for providing less formal recreational and leisure courses. Fees are set by individual further education colleges or local education authorities, which may offer concessions for senior citizens and recipients of welfare benefits.

A wide variety of further education provision for adults is made by a number of voluntary organisations, including the Workers' Educational Association (WEA), and by the BBC and the Open University.

NIACE – the National Organisation for Adult Learning – is the national federal organisation representing the interests of those concerned with adult learning. Its activities include research, development, publications, seminars and conferences.

FURTHER INFORMATION

Addresses

- **Universities and Colleges Admissions Service (UCAS),** Fulton House, Jessop Avenue, Cheltenham GL50 3SH (Tel. 01242 222 444).
- **Open University,** Walton Hall, Milton Keynes MK7 6AA (Tel. 01908 274066).
- **Student Loans Company Ltd,** 100 Bothwell Street, Glasgow G2 7JD (Tel. 0141 306 2000).
- **National Council for Vocational Qualifications,** 222 Euston Road, London NW1 2BZ (Tel. 0171 387 9898).
- **Business and Technology Education Council,** Central House, Upper Woburn Place, London WC1H 0HH (Tel. 0171 413 8400).

- **City and Guilds of London Institute,** 1 Giltspur Street, London EC1A 9DD (Tel. 0171 294 2468).
- **Workers' Educational Association,** Temple House, 17 Victoria Park Square, London E2 9PB (Tel. 0181 983 1515).
- **NIACE (National Organisation of Adult Learning),** 21 De Montfort Street, Leicester LE1 7GE (Tel. 0116 255 1451).
- **Basic Skills Agency,** 7th Floor, Commonwealth House, 1–19 New Oxford Street, London WC1A 1NU (Tel. 0171 405 4017).
- **RSA Examinations Board,** Progress House, Westwood Way, Coventry CV4 8HS (Tel. 01203 470033).
- **Art and Design Admissions Registry,** Penn House, 9 Broad Street, Hereford HR4 9AP (Tel. 01432 26653).

Pensions •

Care for elderly people •

Pensions

State retirement pension • Occupational pensions • Personal pensions •
Other benefits • Further information

What are the pension provisions for elderly people?
The state retirement pension – more usually known as the 'old age
pension' – consists of a basic pension plus, where appropriate, additional
earnings-related payments. The basic pension is a taxable benefit, which
can be paid weekly at a post office, or 4 to 13 weeks in arrears direct to a
bank or building society account. The rates of retirement pension payable
vary depending on the National Insurance contributions paid. An increase
may be payable for a dependent spouse and or dependent children under
19 years of age.

How do you qualify for the basic pension?
The basic pension is currently payable to men at the age of 65 and women
at 60, but in the year 2010 the qualifying age is to be standardised at 65 for
both sexes. The other qualification depends on payment of National
Insurance contributions: these must have been paid at the full rate for
most of the pensioner's working life.

What if you have not paid enough contributions?
People who have not paid enough National Insurance contributions may
get a reduced pension or, in some cases, may not get any pension.
Married women who have not paid full contributions themselves may
claim the married woman's pension when their husbands reach 65 – provided that the husband has himself paid full contributions. Some people
– mothers at home with children, for example, or people who have given
up work to care for sick or disabled relatives – can have their National
Insurance contributions credited so as to safeguard their rights to the
basic pension.

People over 80 may not qualify for the contributory basic pension (National Insurance contributions for the state scheme have only been collected since 1948); they receive the Over-80s Pension – a non-contributory retirement pension.

What if people carry on working after pension age?

Working after pension age does not affect entitlement to the basic pension but if the pension is drawn, it will be counted as part of taxable income. People who carry on working can have their pension payments deferred for up to five years after retirement age, thus increasing their value. People who continue to work after retirement age no longer have to pay National Insurance contributions. Payment of any increases for dependants may be affected if the spouse continues in, or starts in, gainful employment or if they receive an occupational or personal pension of their own.

What are the additions to the basic pension?

If you have paid standard rate National Insurance contributions as an employee after 4 April 1978, you may also get an additional, earnings-related pension. There is also a Graduated Retirement Benefit based on contributions from earnings between April 1961 and April 1975.

What about widows and widowers?

A person whose spouse dies when both were over pensionable age, and who is not already receiving the full basic pension, may be able to use the spouse's contributions to make up the allowance. The surviving spouse can also inherit the husband's or wife's additional pension and half of the graduated pension – provided, again, that both were over pensionable age when the death occurred.

There is a separate Widow's Pension for women aged 55–64 when their husbands died; this pension is not affected by personal earnings. At 60, widows can choose to draw the state retirement pension instead of the widow's pension, and this allows access, where appropriate, to the late husband's graduated pension.

Widows under the age of 60, or those over 60 whose husbands were not entitled to the state retirement pension when they died, receive a tax-free single payment of £1,000 following the death of their husbands, provided their husbands had paid a minimum number of National Insurance contributions.

Women who are aged under 60 years and have a dependent child (or children) for whom they receive Child Benefit may qualify for Widowed Mother's Allowance. Women who were widowed before 11 April 1988 and have a child between 16 and 19 years of age for whom they are not entitled to Child Benefit may be entitled to Widowed Mother's Allowance (Personal).

Women who are widowed between the ages of 45 and 54 will be entitled to a Widow's Pension. The amount payable depends on the woman's age when her husband died or when entitlement to Widowed Mother's Allowance ceased, and the amount of contributions paid by her late husband.

What is an occupational pension?

Some people are 'contracted out' from the state scheme for the additional earnings-related pension by their employers, who provide their own occupational pension scheme instead. This pension must be at least as good as the state additional pension. Occupational pensions do not affect the weekly basic pension, for which the state remains responsible.

What if someone changes jobs before retirement age?

People who change jobs before pensionable age may be able to transfer their occupational pension rights, in which case they have the right to a fair transfer value. If they do not do so, their occupational pension rights are protected against inflation up to a maximum of 5 per cent. The managers of pension schemes have to provide full information about their schemes.

What about personal pensions?

Since 1988 employees have had the right to choose their own personal pension – available from banks, building societies, insurance companies and other financial institutions – instead of staying in the state additional earnings-related scheme or joining an employer's scheme. Again, the weekly state retirement pension is not affected by the existence of a personal pension.

Additional pension will be calculated as though an employee had remained in the state earnings-related pension scheme. The amount of occupational pension and/or personal pension will then be shown as a deduction from the total amount of additional pension calculated.

How are occupational and personal pensions protected?
The Pensions Ombudsman and the Insurance Ombudsman deal with complaints of maladministration and adjudicate on disputes of fact or law. A Pensions Registry, established in 1990, helps people trace lost benefits.

What are the other benefits to which elderly people may be entitled?
For general information about the range of benefits available to help people on low incomes, see sections **Social security and the family, Disablement** and **National Health Service.**

Each year a tax-free Christmas Bonus is automatically paid to people receiving a range of pensions and benefits, including the retirement pension, the Over-80s and Widow's Pensions, Disability Living Allowance, Attendance Allowance and to those of pensionable age on Income Support.

FURTHER INFORMATION

Your local social security office can provide information about pensions and benefits. There is also a free Benefit Enquiry Line (dial 0800 88 22 00).

• *A comprehensive guide, Your Rights 1994–95, by Sally West, is published by* **Age Concern** *and updated every year; contact your local branch of* **Age Concern** *or the* **Age Concern** *headquarters at the address given on p. 123.*

• *For information on War Pensions contact the* **War Pensions Agency,** *DSS, Norcross, Blackpool FY5 3WP. You can also phone the* **War Pensions Helpline** *on 01253 858 858.*

• *For free help and advice on occupational pensions, contact* **Occupational Pensions Advisory Service,** *11 Belgrave Road, London SW1V 1RB.*

Care for elderly people

Home-based support • Getting out of the house • Help to get about •
Sheltered housing • Residential care • Paying for care • Financial management •
Caring for carers • Further information

- **THE NEED FOR CARE** Most elderly people live healthy independent lives as active members of the community. Yet they may have important needs, and some may have particular requirements. Practical support for such people is provided by the local authority social services departments in England and Wales, voluntary organisations such as Age Concern and the Women's Royal Voluntary Service (WRVS), and also the private sector.

What support is available for elderly people living at home?

The Home Help Service, organised by local authorities, provides help with domestic tasks like cleaning and shopping, and increasingly offers more personal care. Voluntary organisations, such as Age Concern and Help the Aged, also provide home-based services, including visiting, shopping and transport.

For elderly people who find cooking difficult, the Meals on Wheels Service provides a hot midday meal delivered directly to their homes. This service is administered by local authorities and often run by the Women's Royal Voluntary Service, the British Red Cross or some Age Concern organisations; a charge is made – usually less than the cost of the food.

Help at home can also be obtained from the private sector. Private firms will provide help at any time of the day or night, holiday relief for a carer or even constant care and companionship for an elderly person. They tend, however, to be expensive and, in some parts of the country, relatively scarce.

What about home maintenance?
Some local authorities run 'Care and Repair' or 'Staying Put' schemes which advise older people on all aspects of repairs and adaptations to their homes, including how to finance the work and how to apply for an improvement grant. Voluntary organisations and community programme workers also do odd jobs, decorating and gardening.

Keeping the house warm is particularly important for older people. Pensioners, whether owner-occupiers or tenants, may get a grant under the Home Energy Efficiency Scheme to help with the cost of draught-proofing and insulation, and local councils may provide other grants to help with installing home heating (see p. 32).

What about getting out of the house?
Older people often find day centres particularly important. Run by local authorities and by voluntary organisations, they offer an opportunity to socialise. Some day centres also provide personal care services such as hair-dressing, chiropody and laundry facilities, or put on art and craft classes or music; others are particularly geared towards rehabilitation and treatment, for people who have had a stroke for instance. There are also some mobile day centres, which cater for the needs of people living in remote rural areas.

Transport to and from day centres (and hospitals) is provided by local authorities, sometimes using their own minibuses, sometimes working through voluntary organisations. For elderly people who cannot use public transport, 'social cars' driven by volunteers enable them to visit the shops, the doctor, family or friends. Other door-to-door transport schemes include Dial-a-Ride, which uses converted cars or minibuses and has to be booked in advance.

For the more mobile, there are concessionary fares for resident pensioners on most bus services, and special discounts are available on coach and rail travel.

What if it's difficult to get about?
Getting about at home can often be made easier by quite minor adaptations – an extra handrail on the stairs, for example, or grips by the bath and lavatory. Grants towards the cost of major alterations, such as fitting a permanent stair lift, may be available from local authorities.

Walking sticks can be bought in local hardware shops and department stores but are sometimes prescribed by the GP or through the hospital. Many community pharmacies have walking sticks, and other aids for daily living, on sale in their stores or would be able to order them from suppliers. Other mobility aids, for example 'zimmer' frames or wheelchairs, are loaned to people with mobility problems through the GP, community or hospital services after assessment by a physiotherapist, who advises on their proper use. The loans can be for short- or long-term use; the range of wheelchairs depends on the locality. Some authorities have agreements with the local Red Cross or similar service to provide standard chairs and these are often very useful for short periods such as holidays or visits to relatives. Electrically-powered wheelchairs or battery-powered vehicles, however, are not supplied free. Older people who receive certain benefits such as the mobility component of the Disability Living Allowance (see p. 98) may be eligible for help towards the cost of buying a wheelchair, scooter or car and having the latter adapted. The independent organisation Motability advises on such matters and helps disabled people obtain adapted cars.

What if living at home becomes too much?
For many elderly people, sheltered housing provides the solution. This accommodation may consist of a group of bungalows or flats, possibly adapted for older residents, usually with some communal facilities. It is often linked by an alarm system to a warden who may live on the premises or who will attend the premises when an alarm is raised. Residents look after themselves but are not responsible for the maintenance of the buildings or the gardens, other than any charges incorporated in rent or leasehold agreements. For older people who need more help, there are now some 'very sheltered housing' schemes. Most sheltered accommodation is provided by local authorities and housing associations.

What if more intensive care is needed?
Residential homes provide full board and, where necessary, personal care. They aim to create a homely and comfortable environment in which residents can live as normally as possible and in which their privacy, independence and personal dignity is respected.

Nursing homes look after people who need round the clock nursing care. A qualified nurse is always on duty. Some homes provide both residential and nursing care. Nursing homes sometimes accept people on a short stay basis, following a spell in hospital for instance. The local authority may provide or fund long-term residential health care for people who are clinically assessed as needing it because of the complexity or intensity of their care needs.

Who runs these homes?

Local authorities, voluntary organisations, housing associations and private companies are all involved in the provision of residential accommodation for older people. Homes run by the local social services departments often have long waiting lists and places may be offered only to people who have lived in the area for some time. Homes run by housing associations, charities or religious bodies are sometimes restricted to members of a particular profession, religion or trade union. All voluntary and private homes must, by law, be registered with the local authority and are subject to independent inspection.

Nursing homes are generally run by voluntary organisations, private individuals or companies, and have to be registered with district health authorities.

How is residential care paid for?

This depends on whether people have entered residential or nursing care before or after 1 April 1993, when new legislation came into effect. Since that date, elderly people wanting to enter residential care but who cannot pay for such care themselves, must have their care needs assessed by the social services department of their local authority. If a place is then offered in a private or voluntary home, the local authority pays the fees and the individual contributes according to income and capital. An elderly person who chooses a different, more expensive home must make arrangements to raise the additional money. If a place is offered in a local authority home, the individual must contribute to the fees if his or her income is at or above the level of the basic pension.

Those already resident in private or voluntary homes on 1 April 1993 continue to receive help with paying fees by means of the special levels of Income Support which formed the basis of the system before the new legislation was passed. Those in local authority homes on 1 April 1993 have had their contributions reassessed.

What if elderly people need help to manage their financial affairs?
If, because of illness or disability, an older person cannot collect his or her pension, he or she may nominate someone (known as the agent) to do so, and must sign a declaration to this effect. If this is to be a long-term arrangement, the local Benefits Agency office can produce an agency card, which shows that the agent named on it is authorised to collect the benefits and hand them over to the pensioner.

If an older person becomes very frail and confused, the Department of Social Security can appoint someone to act on his or her behalf. The appointee (usually a close relative) can collect any benefits due and spend them in the interests of the person concerned.

Power of Attorney
Power of Attorney is an arrangement by which an elderly person (the donor) authorises someone to act on his or her behalf. It is a legal document drawn up by a solicitor, which can only be made when the donor is mentally competent and able to supervise the attorney's actions; it can be used in dealing with banks, insurance companies, pension funds and similar bodies.

Enduring Power of Attorney, which must also be granted when the donor is mentally competent, makes provision for the future when this may no longer be the case.

Where no such power exists, the Court of Protection can give directions about the estates of people who are no longer capable of managing their own affairs: this is often done by appointing a receiver – usually a relative or a solicitor and accountable to the Court – to deal with the person's affairs.

Is there any help for carers?
Friends and relatives involved in the day-to-day care of an elderly person may need to have a break from this task. The Crossroads Care Attendance scheme, jointly funded by local authorities and district health authorities, provides trained care attendants who can take over the role of carer so that the usual carer has some free time. Some Age Concern groups also run a similar service.

Respite care for older people can also be provided on a daily basis in day centres. To give a carer a longer break, some residential homes offer accommodation for elderly people on a short-term basis; in some areas fostering schemes arrange for an older person to stay for a short time with a family. The Carers' National Association provides advice and information and acts as a national pressure group representing the needs of carers.

FURTHER INFORMATION

For services provided by your local authority, contact your local social services department, listed in the phone book. The local branch of the **British Red Cross, Women's Royal Voluntary Service, Age Concern** and **Help the Aged** will be able to tell you what services they offer and any publications they produce. Your doctor's surgery, local library and Citizens Advice Bureau are also sources of help and information.

Addresses
• **Age Concern**
England: 1268 London Road, London SW16 4ER.
Wales: 4th Floor, 1 Cathedral Road, Cardiff CF1 9SD.
• **Carers' National Association,** Ruth Pitter House, 20–25 Glasshouse Yard, London EC1A 4JS.

• **Carers' Helpline:** Tel. 0171 490 8898 (Monday to Friday 1–4pm).
• **Counsel and Care for the Elderly** (a free advisory service for older people), Twyman House, 16 Bonny Street, London NW1 9PG (Tel. 0171 485 1550).
• **Help the Aged,** St James's Walk, London EC1R 0BE (Tel. 0171 253 0253).
• **Motability,** Gate House, West Gate, Harlow, Essex CM20 1HR (Tel. 01279 635666).
• **Women's Royal Voluntary Service National Headquarters,** 234–244 Stockwell Road, London SW9 9SP (Tel. 0171 416 1046).

Legal aid, law centres •
and Citizens Advice Bureaux

The police and the citizen •

Court service •

Legal aid, law centres and Citizens Advice Bureaux

Legal advice and assistance • Civil legal aid • Duty solicitor • Criminal legal aid •

Law centres and legal advice centres • Citizens Advice Bureaux •

Further information

There are three kinds of legal aid: legal advice and assistance, civil legal aid and criminal legal aid.

To apply for legal aid you must first see a solicitor. Libraries, town halls and most advice centres will have a copy of the Solicitor's Regional Directory, where you will find a list of most local solicitors and the type of work they cover. You can also go to any solicitor's office displaying the legal aid sign, or enquire at your local Citizens Advice Bureau or law centre.

You will need to give your solicitor accurate information about your financial position, including details of your partner's finances; these will be included in the assessment of your means, unless you live apart or there is a conflict of interest between you. Legal aid may be taken away from you if you give your solicitor false information. Make sure you tell your solicitor if your financial position, or your address, changes.

- **LEGAL ADVICE AND ASSISTANCE** Legal advice and assistance (also known as the 'Green Form scheme') is available in England and Wales. It covers general advice from a solicitor on almost any point of English law and may include help in areas such as writing letters, negotiating, getting a barrister's opinion and preparing a written case if you have to go before a tribunal. This help can cover most legal problems such as divorce or maintenance, and, in certain circumstances, the making of a will. The Green Form scheme enables people to get free assistance from a solicitor until his or her charges reach a total of two hours' work, although the solicitor may apply for an extension of this time. If you wish to apply for legal advice and assistance, your solicitor will fill in an application form and will tell you immediately if you qualify. You will not have to pay a contribution.

Assistance by Way of Representation (ABWOR) covers the cost of a solicitor preparing your case and representing you in most civil cases in magistrates' courts. This may include cases such as separation, maintenance (except child maintenance where the Child Support Agency has jurisdiction), paternity and defended adoption proceedings. It is also available for prisoners facing disciplinary charges before the prison governor, discretionary lifers whose cases are being referred to the Parole Board and for patients appearing before Mental Health Review Tribunals.

If you want to apply for ABWOR, your solicitor will fill in an application form and send it to the Legal Aid Office. They will decide if you qualify. If your application is refused, you have the right to appeal. If you do qualify for ABWOR, you may have to pay a contribution towards the cost, depending on your income and savings. You should also remember that if anything is recovered or preserved in your case under Green Form or ABWOR, it may have to be put towards paying your solicitor's bill.

- **CIVIL LEGAL AID** Civil legal aid is available for civil cases in the House of Lords, the High Court and Court of Appeal, county courts (with some exceptions), the Employment Appeal Tribunal, the Lands Tribunal, the Commons Commissioners and in some cases the Restrictive Practices Court. It is also given for cases in Family Proceedings Courts concerning marriage and the family, with the exception of those cases covered by Assistance by Way of Representation. It is not available for proceedings before a coroner's court.

Civil legal aid in these cases covers all the work leading up to and including the court proceedings and representation by a solicitor and, if necessary, a barrister. To apply for civil legal aid, you should ask your solicitor to help you fill in the application forms and send them to the Legal Aid Office. (Your solicitor can be paid for this work if you qualify for legal aid and assistance.) If you qualify financially, the assessment officer will inform the Legal Aid Office, who decides if your application satisfies criteria known as the merits test. You must show you have reasonable grounds for taking, defending or being a party to proceedings, and that it is reasonable to grant you legal aid in all the circumstances of the case. If your application is refused you will have the right to appeal.

If your case is urgent, your solicitor can ask for emergency legal aid. This can be granted immediately. Emergency legal aid lasts only until a decision has been taken on your full application for civil legal aid. When you apply for emergency legal aid, you must agree to co-operate with the assessment officer in his or her enquiry into your financial position and also to pay any contribution that is assessed. You also have to agree to pay the full costs of your case if it is found that you do not qualify for civil legal aid, or if you refuse it when it is offered to you because you are being asked to pay a contribution.

If your application for civil legal aid is successful, you may be asked to make a contribution towards your legal costs. If so, the Legal Aid Office will send you an offer of a Legal Aid certificate, explaining how much you will be expected to pay. Should you recover or preserve any property as a result of the proceedings, *and* if the other side does not pay your costs in full, the Legal Aid Office will deduct from you as much as may be needed to cover those costs. If you lose your case, you will usually only have to pay the contribution due under your certificate. However, the court may decide that you should pay your opponent's expenses; this is not covered by legal aid. The court will assess how much you should pay according to your means and your conduct in connection with the dispute.

- **DUTY SOLICITOR** If the police question you about an offence, you have the right to free legal advice. There is no means test for such advice. You may ask for your own solicitor, the 24-hour duty solicitor, or choose a solicitor from the list kept by the police.

If you have to go to the magistrates' court on a criminal case, there will usually be a duty solicitor available either at the court or on call to give you free advice and representation on your first appearance. There is, again, no means test. Ask the court staff for the duty solicitor.

- **CRIMINAL LEGAL AID** You may apply for criminal legal aid if you have been charged with a criminal offence. This will cover solicitor's costs for preparing your defence and representing you in court (and the costs of a barrister if necessary), and also advice on appeal against a verdict or sentence of the magistrates' court or the Crown Court and preparing the notice of appeal. It may also be available for bail application.

To apply for criminal legal aid you should ask your solicitor to fill in the forms and send them to the court where your case will be heard. You will need to give the solicitor written details of the criminal charge against you and your financial position. To qualify, the court must decide that you need help to pay the costs of your case *and* that it is in the 'interests of justice' that you should have legal representation. The court may decide that it is in the 'interests of justice' to grant you criminal legal aid where, for example, your case is so serious that if you are found guilty you are likely to go to prison or lose your job; or where there are substantial questions of law to be argued; or if you are unable to follow the proceedings and explain your case because you do not speak English or you are mentally ill. If the court decides that you qualify, you may be asked to pay a contribution towards the cost, depending on your income and savings.

If you are refused criminal legal aid, you may be able to appeal against the decision. In any case, a solicitor may still be able to give you some help preparing your own case for court under the legal advice and assistance scheme.

- **LAW CENTRES** In some urban areas law centres provide free legal advice and representation. They may employ a salaried lawyer and many have community workers. Much of their time is devoted to housing, employment and social security problems. Although there is a restriction on cases they will accept, most law centres will give preliminary advice.

- **LEGAL ADVICE CENTRES** Legal advice centres mainly provide advice, and any further assistance they can offer is limited. They are staffed mainly by volunteer lawyers. Citizens Advice Bureaux will have details of local legal advice centres.

- **CITIZENS ADVICE BUREAUX** Citizens Advice Bureaux give free, confidential, impartial and independent advice and information on a wide range of subjects such as debt and consumer problems, housing matters, legal queries and employment problems. If they cannot give the help needed they will direct the client to the appropriate professional body.

FURTHER INFORMATION

To find out about Legal Aid for England and Wales, contact the **Legal Aid Board,** 29–37 Red Lion Street, London WC1R 4PN. *You can contact the* **Law Centres Federation** *at* Duchess House, 18–19 Warren Street, London W1P 5DB (Tel. 0171 387 8570).

The National Association of Citizens Advice Bureaux *(NACAB) can be contacted at* Myddelton House, 115–123 Pentonville Road, London N1 9LZ (Tel. 0171 833 2181).

The police and the citizen

Co-operating with the police • Stop and search • Arrest and detention •
Rights to bail • Searching property • Police complaints • Further information

The public duties of the police include the prevention and detection of crime, keeping public order, helping the public and providing an emergency 999 service. Full information on the law relating to police powers and duties in England and Wales is found in the Police and Criminal Evidence Act 1984 (PACE). This Act is supplemented by a number of Codes of Practice relating to specific areas of police work.

- **DO I HAVE TO CO-OPERATE WITH THE POLICE?** There is no law which states that you must help the police with their enquiries. If you refuse to help the police, no action can be taken against you unless you are found guilty of giving misleading information or wasting police time. The police cannot make someone accompany them to the police station unless they arrest him or her. If you go to the police station of your own free will to help the police with their enquiries, you are free to go at any time unless you are arrested.

- **CAN THE POLICE STOP AND SEARCH ME?** The police do not have a general right to stop and search anybody. However, any police officer does have the right to stop and search an individual if they have 'reasonable grounds' for suspecting that the person is carrying certain forbidden items such as offensive weapons, tools that could be used to commit burglary, or illegal drugs. Under the Criminal Justice and Public Order Act 1994, police officers also have powers of stop and search in anticipation of violence. If you are searched you should be told on what grounds. The officer should identify himself or herself and the police station he or she is attached to. A written record should be made of the details of the search, including the grounds for suspicion, time and date. A police officer can use reasonable force as a last resort.

- **POLICE POWERS OF ARREST** In practice the police have wide powers to arrest suspects with or without a warrant issued by a court. They have the power to arrest without a warrant when a person is committing, or is suspected of having committed, an arrestable offence. Arrestable offences cover all offences for which a sentence of five years' imprisonment or more can be imposed. Arrest without a warrant also applies to people suspected of committing serious arrestable offences such as murder, rape and kidnapping. For lesser offences, arrest without warrant exists if it is not possible or appropriate to send out a summons to appear in court. The police must have reasonable grounds for an arrest and they have to inform an arrested person of those grounds.

- **WHAT WILL HAPPEN IF I AM ARRESTED?** You can only be detained at a police station if you have been arrested. Once arrested, you must be taken to the station as soon as is practicable. You have the right to see a solicitor and to have one other person informed of your arrest (see below). You also have the right to look at the code of practice setting out the rules of police conduct applying to the treatment and questioning of detainees.

The police in England and Wales must caution you before questioning, as follows:

'You do not have to say anything. But it may harm your defence if you do not mention when questioned something which you later rely on in court. Anything you do say may be given in evidence.'

The courts may draw an inference from a refusal to answer questions.

- **HOW LONG CAN I BE DETAINED WITHOUT CHARGE?** The time a suspect is held in police custody before charge is strictly regulated. For lesser offences this may not exceed 24 hours in England and Wales. Someone suspected of committing a serious arrestable offence can be detained for up to 96 hours without charge, but only beyond 36 hours if a warrant is obtained from a magistrates' court. Reviews must be made of a person's detention at regular intervals to check whether the criteria for detention are still satisfied. If they are not, the person must be released.

- **WHEN CAN I SEE A SOLICITOR?** All suspects have the right to see a solicitor once they have been detained at a police station. You are free to choose any solicitor you want; but if you do not know one or cannot get hold of one, there should always be a duty solicitor on call who is independent from the police and whose services are provided free through the legal aid system (see p.128).

For serious arrestable offences the police can delay access to a solicitor on the grounds that it may alert other unarrested suspects, interfere with the evidence or hinder the recovery of stolen property.

- **WHO ELSE CAN I CONTACT?** You may contact a friend or family member at public expense to tell him or her that you are being detained. If that particular person cannot be contacted you can choose up to two alternatives. The police can delay this right if the suspected offence is a serious arrestable offence on the same grounds as given for the power to delay seeing a solicitor (see above).

- **MUST I AGREE TO BEING SEARCHED?** Once you have been arrested and detained at a police station the police have wider powers of search. First, a basic search may be made to enable the custody officer to ascertain what property you have with you, and all the items in your possession are written down. You then sign this document. Reasonable force can be used to search a person who has been arrested and is in the police station. If the police want to carry out a strip search, they must give reasons and write them down in the custody record. This type of search is governed by a number of safeguards designed to minimise the embarrassment of the person searched. An intimate body search can only be carried out if there are reasonable grounds for believing that certain illegal drugs or a dangerous weapon may be concealed. It may only be authorised by an officer of the rank of superintendent or above.

- **FINGERPRINTS, PHOTOGRAPHS, SAMPLES AND IDENTITY PARADES** The police can take your fingerprints without consent prior to charge if an officer of the rank of superintendent or above reasonably believes that it is necessary to confirm or disprove your involvement in an offence. Once you have been charged with an offence, the police can use force to take fingerprints. If you are later acquitted, the fingerprints must be destroyed. Your fingerprints may also be taken without consent if you have been convicted of a recordable offence. The police can take photographs without consent in certain circumstances, although force may not be used.

The police may take non-intimate body samples without consent from anyone who is detained or convicted for a recordable offence. The samples can be used to search against existing records of convicted offenders or unsolved crimes. Intimate body samples cannot be taken without a suspect's consent.

You have the right to refuse to take part in an identity parade but if you do so the police can arrange an informal identification. You have the right to have a solicitor or friend present at the identification parade.

- **WILL I BE RELEASED ON BAIL?** The court decides whether a defendant should be released on bail. The only grounds for withholding unconditional bail are that the accused would abscond, commit an offence, interfere with witnesses or otherwise obstruct the course of justice. A court may impose conditions before granting bail. If bail is refused, you may apply to a High Court judge or to the Crown Court for bail.

- **CAN THE POLICE ENTER MY HOME?** The police can enter and search your home if they have consent or if they have a search warrant. A search warrant is issued by a magistrates' court for suspected serious offences only. The police can also search without consent and without a warrant:
- to make an arrest;
- stop someone getting hurt;
- look for drugs; or
- to catch an escaped prisoner.

The police can use reasonable force to make a lawful search.

Any property seized by the police should be material evidence or the proceeds of a crime. There are certain categories of evidence that cannot

be removed without an order from a Crown Court Judge, such as communications between clients and their lawyers or confidential records held by
third parties (for example, social workers' records). If you think that any
property was taken without proper authority, you can apply to the magistrates' court for a court order for its return.

• **HOW DO I MAKE A COMPLAINT OF ALLEGED POLICE MIS-
CONDUCT?** You can make a complaint against a police officer if you feel
that you have been treated unfairly or improperly. This can be done by
contacting the duty officer at the local police station, writing to the chief
constable, or by going through a solicitor. You can also write to the independent Police Complaints Authority (which oversees the investigation
and resolution of complaints in England and Wales – see also p. 166), who
will forward the complaint to the police for investigation. If the complaint
is upheld, the police officer or officers may face disciplinary action and
could be prosecuted if criminal offences have occurred.

FURTHER INFORMATION

The **Police Complaints Authority** for England
and Wales can be contacted at 10 Great George
Street, London SW1P 3AE (Tel. 0171 273 6450).

Court service

Jury service • Being a witness • Courts Charter • Being a magistrate •
Further information

Law in Britain is formulated and enforced on behalf of the people, and there is a long tradition of the general public participating in its process.

- **JURY SERVICE** In England and Wales a jury comprises 12 lay people, sworn to decide the facts of a case and reach a verdict in a court of law. Juries are implemented primarily in criminal cases, but also sometimes in civil cases – for example, inquests and defamation trials.

  In serious criminal trials, the presiding judge decides questions of law and sums up the evidence for the jury, whose verdict may be 'guilty' or 'not guilty'. If the jury cannot reach a unanimous decision, the judge may allow a 10–2 majority verdict.

  A jury in a civil case decides questions of fact and determines the damages to be paid to the injured party; majority verdicts may be accepted.

- **ELIGIBILITY** People between the ages of 18 and 70 whose names appear on the electoral register, with certain exceptions, are liable for jury service. Ineligible people include, for example, judges, police officers and solicitors. People convicted of certain offences may be disqualified. It is an offence if you sit on a jury when ineligible or disqualified, or if you fail to attend for jury service without good reason.

- **BEING SUMMONED** Potential jurors are chosen at random by computer from names on the electoral register. If you are selected, you will receive a summons giving the date and other relevant details of your attendance, and information about court procedure.

You can ask to be excused from jury service if your personal circumstances would make jury duty particularly difficult, for example, if a disability would make it hard to follow court proceedings, or if you have special holiday or work commitments (although in such cases you may be asked to appear at another time). If your reasons are not accepted, you can appeal to the jury summoning officer in writing at the court you have been assigned to. A judge will then decide whether the appeal can be granted without a formal hearing. Where a hearing is necessary, you will be notified of the hearing date.

- **LENGTH OF SERVICE** Jury service usually lasts for a minimum of five working days but can continue up to, and over, ten working days. If a trial looks likely to last an unusually long time, you will be asked at court if this presents difficulties for you. If you are serving as a juror and fall ill, or something happens which prevents you from continuing as a juror, you must inform the jury summoning officer without delay.

You are not paid for jury duty but you can claim expenses such as travel expenses and loss of earnings subject to a maximum daily amount.

- **BEING A WITNESS** If you are a witness to a crime or other serious incident, or are the victim of crime, you may give your account to your local police force. But you may have to go to court and give your evidence in person, especially if a defendant pleads not guilty.

If you have to attend court, and you are a witness for the prosecution, you will be notified by the police of the likely dates that the case may come to court. If you are a witness for the defence, you will be contacted by the defendant's solicitor. If the proposed dates are particularly difficult for you, contact the witness liaison officer at the court immediately. When the date for a trial is fixed, witnesses will be informed by either the police or the defendant's solicitor, and are then legally required to attend. The court can take action against witnesses who do not attend to give evidence without a good reason.

You do not get paid for being a witness, but can claim the same expenses as jurors (see p. 137).

- **COURT PROCEDURE** Witnesses are not admitted to the particular court where they are to give their evidence until they are called by a court usher. After entering the witness box you will be asked to take the oath or affirm. You must answer questions truthfully or you risk prosecution for perjury. During the giving of evidence, witnesses may ask for permission to refer to notes.

- **VICTIMS AND CHILD WITNESSES** Special provision is made for witnesses giving evidence who are victims or children. The Crown Court Witness Service, which provides support for victims, can be contacted through your local police station. In certain circumstances children may be able to give their evidence via a live television link from a private room, without having to enter the courtroom.

- **COURTS CHARTER** A Courts Charter, setting out the standards of service which apply in the higher courts in England and Wales, came into operation in January 1993, outlining arrangements to help court users and ease the strains associated with court attendance.

From July 1995 a new Charter, known as the 'Charter for Court Users', sets out the minimum standards of service and business performance court users can expect from the Crown Court, county courts and the High Court in England and Wales. The Charter also tells court users what to do if something goes wrong. Copies can be obtained from your local court or from Customer Service Unit, Room 6.59, Lord Chancellor's Department, Southside, 105 Victoria Street, London SW1E 6QT (Tel. 0171 210 1676/1689).

- **BEING A MAGISTRATE** In England and Wales summary offences – the less serious offences and the vast majority of criminal cases – are not tried by jury but are heard in magistrates' courts. A magistrates' court usually consists of a bench of three lay magistrates – also known as justices of the peace (JPs) – who are advised on points of law and procedure by a legally qualified clerk or a qualified assistant. Where magistrates consider a case to be too serious for them to deal with, they may commit an accused person to the Crown Court for trial.

There are over 30,000 lay magistrates, who are unpaid but may receive certain allowances to cover expenses incurred in their duties. They must be prepared to sit at least 26 times a year.

- **APPOINTMENT AS A MAGISTRATE** Lay magistrates are recommended for the job by committees of local people; when new magistrates are needed, the committees seek nominations from local organisations or businesses. If you wish to nominate yourself contact your local magistrates' court, which will be able to put you in touch with the local advisory committee and provide further information on the selection process. The local committee is expected to make sure that magistrates are drawn from many walks of life and that the composition of the bench is broadly balanced. Most are appointed by the Lord Chancellor and the remainder by the Chancellor of the Duchy of Lancaster.

- **TRAINING** Lay magistrates must complete an initial training programme where their duties are explained, court procedures practised, and basic points of law studied. Special training is given to those magistrates who deal with juveniles or family matters. Training continues during the first three years of their appointment. In addition, lay magistrates undergo refresher courses.

FURTHER INFORMATION

*Explanatory information for jurors (*You and your Jury Service for England and Wales*) should accompany every jury summons. For more information on court procedure for witnesses, see the leaflet* Witness in Court. *Information on becoming a magistrate can be found in the booklets* Today's Magistrate – The Work of Magistrates in England and Wales *and* Justices of the Peace in England and Wales – Their Appointment and Duties Explained. *Both guidance leaflets and booklets can be obtained from your local court, listed in your local phone book under Courts.*

The Crown Court Witness Service can be contacted either through your local court or through Victim Support. The Victim Support head office is at Cranmer House, 39 Brixton Road, London SW9 6DZ (Tel. 0171 735 9166).

Consumer rights •

British Standards and •
safety marks

Consumer rights

- **GOODS** The law says that goods must:

- 'be of satisfactory quality' – this covers, for example, their appearance and finish, their safety and durability; goods must be free from defects, even minor ones, except when they have been brought to your attention by the seller, such as if the goods are said to be shop soiled;

- 'be fit for their purpose, including any particular purpose mentioned by you to the seller'; and

- 'be as described' (on the package or display sign, or by the seller).

These are your statutory rights. All goods bought or hired from a trader – from a shop, street market, catalogue or doorstep seller – are covered by these rights. This includes goods bought in sales. When you buy something, you and the seller make a contract, even if all you do is talk. The seller, not the manufacturer, must sort out any complaint you might have.

If you tell the seller promptly that goods are faulty and you do not want them, you should be able to get your money back. You may be offered a replacement, free repair or credit note, but you do not have to accept. Do not delay in examining what you have bought or in telling the seller about a fault. You are entitled to a reasonable time to examine goods. If you keep them after that time without complaining, you may lose your right to a full refund, and will usually have to accept an offer to have the goods put right, or the cost of a repair.

A reasonable time to examine goods is not fixed – it depends on the circumstances. But normally you can at least take the goods home and try them out. If you sign an acceptance note when you receive goods, you still have a reasonable time to examine them.

If you receive goods as a present and they turn out to be faulty, it is up to the person who bought them to return them to the seller. The buyer has the contract with the seller. Many shops, however, will deal with your complaint providing you have some proof of purchase.

You are not legally obliged to return faulty goods to the seller at your own expense. If an item would be difficult or expensive to return, ask the seller to collect it. This does not apply if you have had the goods for some time, or been given them as a present.

You may be able to claim compensation if you suffer loss because of faulty goods – for example, if clothes are damaged by a faulty iron.

If you complain about faulty goods you do not need a receipt, although it is useful evidence of when and where the purchase was made.

You are not entitled to anything if you:
- examined the goods when you bought them and should have seen the fault;
- were told about the fault;
- simply changed your mind;
- made a mistake when you bought the goods; or
- did any damage yourself.

In these circumstances, many shops will help out of goodwill.

- **SERVICES** When you pay for a service – for instance, from a dry cleaner or travel agent – you are entitled to certain standards. Anyone providing a service must do so:
- 'with reasonable care and skill' – the job should be done to a proper standard of workmanship;

- 'within a reasonable time' – even if you have not agreed a definite completion time with the supplier; and

- 'for a reasonable charge, if no price has been fixed in advance'. If the price was fixed at the outset, or some other way of working out the charge was agreed, you cannot complain later that it is unreasonable.

Always ask how much a job will cost. The trader may only be able to make an informed guess and give you an estimate. If you agree a fixed cost it is usually called a quotation. A fixed price is binding whatever it is called. Where materials or goods are used in the provision of a service, the materials or goods are covered by the law in the same way as when you buy them directly.

- **MAKING A COMPLAINT** Go back to the shop as soon as possible, taking the goods with you if you can. If you cannot get to the shop quickly, telephone instead. For services, contact the company, giving it the chance to put things right. Take the receipt or other proof of purchase, such as a credit card slip or cheque stub, if you have one. Ask for the manager, explain the problem and say what you want done.

If you are not satisfied with the outcome, write to the customer services manager or the chairman at the head office if there is one. If you still do not get anywhere, get further help (see p. 145).

If you phone, have the relevant receipts or documents ready. Get the name of the person you speak to, making a note of the time and date and what is said. If you write, use special/recorded postal delivery so you can easily check that your letter has been delivered. Keep copies of anything you send. Do not send original documents like receipts and guarantees – send copies.

- **BUYING ON CREDIT** If a trader has an arrangement with a finance or credit card company to allow you to pay by credit, you have extra protection. This applies if the goods cost more than £100, even if you only pay a deposit. The credit card company is equally liable for any claim you have against the trader for breach of contract or misrepresentation. For example, if the goods are not delivered or are not what you ordered, or are faulty, you may be able to claim from the credit card or finance company.

- **WHO CAN HELP?** Free help and advice is available from the following sources:

- trading standards (or consumer protection) departments, which are part of the local authority and which investigate false or misleading descriptions or prices, inaccurate weights and measures and some aspects of the safety of goods. They often advise on shopping problems, and some run consumer advice centres in main shopping centres;

- Citizens Advice Bureaux, which give advice on consumer problems and going to court;

- environmental health departments, which are also part of the local authority and deal with health matters such as unfit food and drink, and dirty shops and restaurants; and

- trade associations, some of which have codes of practice covering standards and how to deal with complaints. Some also have low-cost conciliation or arbitration schemes.

- **GOING TO COURT** If all else fails, you can go to court to sue for the return of your money or for compensation. If your claim is for £1,000 or less, you can use the small claims procedure. This is quite informal and usually held in private, without solicitors. Even if you lose you will not have to pay your opponent's legal costs. Forms and information booklets are available from the court office (look under Courts in the phone book for the address) and Citizens Advice Bureaux. Some bookshops sell advice packs which include the forms.

- **MORE ON YOUR RIGHTS**

Safety

It is an offence for a supplier to sell goods unless they are safe. This applies to both new and second-hand goods, but not to antiques or goods needing repair or reconditioning, provided you were clearly informed of this fact. If you believe that you have bought unsafe goods, contact your trading standards department.

Auctions

Auctioneers can refuse to be responsible for faulty goods, so you may have fewer rights than when you buy in a shop. Check any notices and catalogues for exclusion clauses and conditions of sale.

Second-hand goods

When you buy second-hand from a trader, you have the same rights as when you buy new goods, but bear in mind that second-hand may not be the same quality as new. You can claim your money back if the goods are faulty, unless it is a matter of wear and tear to be expected with second-hand items, or the fault was obvious or was pointed out to you before you paid.

Buying privately

You have fewer rights if you buy privately. Goods only have to be as described. Your rights depend on what is said about the value and condition of the goods. Take someone with you as a witness.

Exclusion clauses

Some traders may try to escape their responsibilities for faulty goods by using exclusion clauses. For example, a shop may display a sign saying 'no refunds given'. Making a statement like this about goods is an offence. Similar statements about services – for instance, 'no responsibility for loss or damage, however caused' printed on the back of a dry-cleaning ticket – are not illegal and may be valid in certain circumstances. But if a clause is unfair it has no legal force. Only a court can decide what is fair.

Goods on order

If you order goods, you can arrange a date by which you must have them. If they do not arrive by then you can cancel your order. If you do not arrange a fixed date, the seller must still deliver in a reasonable time. If you think enough time has passed, tell the seller that if the goods have not arrived by a certain date (perhaps within 14 days), you want your money back. But if you agree at that point to wait longer, you cannot cancel in that time.

When you order goods you should arrange a fixed price with the seller. You may agree to pay the extra if the price goes up before delivery. Make sure you know where you stand – preferably in writing.

Deposits

If you pay a deposit and cancel your order, the seller may be able to keep your deposit and claim damages. Check whether a deposit is refundable and, if so, in what circumstances.

Guarantees

A guarantee can be a useful back-up if you have to complain. This is in addition to, not instead of, your legal rights. With some goods, you get a manufacturer's guarantee but it is still up to the seller to deal with your complaint.

You may be offered an extended guarantee or warranty, for which you may have to pay, when you buy expensive goods such as a washing machine or television. Check exactly what the warranty covers, and remember that the peace of mind it gives is unlikely to be good value for money.

Manufacturers cannot use guarantees to limit their liability for loss or damage where this results from a defect in their products caused by their negligence.

Do not choose a firm just because they guarantee their work. A ten-year guarantee is useless if the firm has gone out of business. Insurance-backed guarantees may offer extra protection.

Misleading prices and untrue claims

It is a criminal offence for traders to make misleading price claims about goods or services. For example, 'was £120 – now £99.99' is misleading if the goods were never on sale at the higher price. Similarly, untrue claims are illegal – if a trader promises a 24-hour service, this must be true. If you feel you have been seriously misled, tell your local trading standards department, which may be able to investigate.

FURTHER INFORMATION

The Office of Fair Trading has a range of free publications giving consumer advice. A list is available from

Office of Fair Trading, P.O. Box 2, Central Way, Feltham, Middlesex TW14 0TG (Tel. 0181 398 3405).

British Standards and safety marks

British Standards • The British Standards Institution • Identifying a product approved by the BSI • Other safety marks • Complaining about unsafe products • Further information

- **WHAT ARE BRITISH STANDARDS?** British Standards (BS) are technical documents that lay down national standards for industrial and consumer products. They are issued for voluntary adoption, though in some cases compliance with a British Standard is required by legislation. Each document has a separate number – for example, BS 5665 is the standard for toy safety, BS 1363 for 13 amp electrical plugs. There are cases where more than one standard may apply. For instance, there are two British Standards applicable to kitchens – BS 3705 covers the space, design and layout and BS 3456 covers specifications for the safety of electrical appliances. There are more than 10,000 British Standards. They are changed whenever necessary and fully reviewed every five years.

  Standards are becoming more and more harmonised with Europe and worldwide, and BS numbers are being changed to indicate their provenance. For example, BS 3456 (above) is now dual-numbered as BSEN 60335.

- **WHO SETS THESE STANDARDS?** British Standards are prepared by the independent British Standards Institution (BSI). In consultation with the interests concerned, BSI sets standards relating to nearly every sector of Britain's industry and trade. It also represents Britain at European and other international standards meetings.

- **HOW DO I IDENTIFY A PRODUCT APPROVED BY THE BSI?** There are accompanying certification marks to look for on products to show that they have been independently approved by the BSI itself.

Where products carry only a BS number, it is solely the manufacturer's claim that the goods comply with the relevant British Standard. They will not have been independently tested by the BSI, nor will they have been manufactured under a quality system agreed between the BSI and the manufacturer.

Products which have been tested by the BSI and certified as complying with the relevant British Standard may carry the Institution's certification trade marks, known as the Kitemark and the Safety Mark.

- **OTHER SAFETY MARKS** If a product does not carry a BS number and/or a BSI certification mark, it does not necessarily mean that its safety is suspect. The manufacturer may apply other marks, offering an assurance to the consumer that their product conforms to a safety standard where certification is by another body. For example, many electrical appliances carry a British Electrical Approvals Board (BEAB) certification mark.

Other products may carry an E mark, which shows that they comply with the Economic Commission for Europe's regulations. Since 1990, toys must have the CE mark displayed on them, showing that they meet the requirements of European Community Directives. However, there is no requirement to have the toys independently checked and tested, and it is only the maker's claim that, in their opinion, their toys meet these requirements. Thus, the CE mark is not intended as consumer information but rather as an indication to enforcement officers. CE marks are beginning to appear on other products such as gas and electric appliances.

If you are buying a particular type of product and are unsure what standard mark to look for, you can enquire at the trading standards department of your local authority.

- **COMPLAINING ABOUT UNSAFE PRODUCTS** If you are concerned about the safety of a product, contact your local trading standards department. Trading standards officers have the power to seize dangerous goods, stop them from being sold, and may initiate legal proceedings to ban products.

FURTHER INFORMATION

The **British Standards Institution** produces a range of free and paid-for leaflets and booklets on British Standards and safety. For details contact **Communications Group**, BSI, 389 Chiswick High Road, London W4 4AL.

Personal tax and •
National Insurance

Debt •

Personal tax and National Insurance

Income tax • PAYE • Tax returns and assessment • Other taxes • Council tax •
Advice and complaints • National Insurance • Further information

Levels of taxation are set by the Government and may be revised each year in the Budget.

• **INCOME TAX** If you have income of any kind – wages, salary, pension payments or interest on investments you may be liable to pay income tax (although some kinds of income are exempt, such as certain social security benefits). Larger incomes bear a proportionately greater amount of tax.

A number of allowances and reliefs reduce the amount of your taxable income compared with gross income. Every taxpayer, irrespective of sex or marital status, is entitled to a personal tax allowance, that is, the amount you can earn in a tax year (6 April one year to 5 April the next) before starting to pay tax. Married women pay their own tax on the basis of their own income. There is a married couple's allowance, which may be allocated to either partner or they may receive half each. There is also a tax relief for mortgage interest payments on borrowing (up to a statutory limit) for buying your own home.

• **PAYE** If you work for an employer, your tax will be deducted from your wages or salary through Pay-As-You-Earn (PAYE). Your payslip will tell you how much tax has been deducted and what your tax code is. This code, comprising letters and numbers, is based on the reliefs and allowances you are eligible for. If you do not understand your code, or think it is wrong, contact your tax office, giving them your tax reference number, National Insurance number (see p. 154) and name and address of your employer.

Self-employed people do not come under the umbrella of PAYE as they do not pay tax on money as they earn it.

If you are an employer, you can get guidance on operating PAYE from your PAYE tax office – including two booklets *Employer's basic guide to PAYE (P8)* and *Employer's further guide to PAYE (P7)*.

- **TAX RETURNS AND ASSESSMENT** You must provide the Inland Revenue with a full statement of your income from whatever source. The Revenue may send you a tax return, which must be completed within a specified period. Each tax return comes with an accompanying explanatory guide. You may not receive a return if your tax affairs are straightforward. However, you may still need to complete one if there has been a change in your entitlement to an allowance or relief, if you have received income which the Revenue does not know about, or if you think you have paid too much tax and want to claim a rebate.

If you receive a tax assessment from the Inland Revenue which says you have paid too much tax, you will get a rebate with perhaps some interest. If the assessment says you have underpaid, you will have to pay the outstanding balance and possibly some interest. If you are an employee, the underpayment can be recovered through the PAYE system. If you get an assessment which you think is wrong, you have the chance to appeal within a certain period (see the leaflet *Income tax and CGT – appeals*).

- **OTHER TAXES** Other taxes which you may pay include:
- inheritance tax, which may be charged on the value of an estate when someone dies (although it is not applicable to transfers between husband and wife in a will);
- capital gains tax, which may be charged on any gains you make when you sell an asset (for example, shares or land);
- stamp duties, payable on certain kinds of transfers including purchases of houses; and
- expenditure taxes, such as value added tax (VAT) and customs and excise duties.

- **COUNCIL TAX** The amount of council tax you pay to your local government authority depends on the valuation band placed on the property in which you live, either as owner or tenant. Every dwelling is allocated one of eight valuation bands, based on its capital value in April 1991. The higher the band the more tax you will pay. You may be able to get a reduction in council tax in some circumstances, such as if you live on your own or if you are receiving benefits. Contact your local council for more information.

- **ADVICE AND COMPLAINTS** Your local tax office or enquiry centre will help you with most everyday tax queries and problems. However if your tax affairs are particularly complex, or you want to engage in detailed tax planning, or if you are self-employed, it may be advisable to get help from an accountant, taxation consultant or solicitor.

The Taxpayer's Charter sets out the standard of service that you can expect from the Inland Revenue and from HM Customs and Excise (which collects VAT and excise duties). Both departments should be fair, helpful, courteous, efficient and accountable, and keep taxpayers' financial affairs private.

If you feel that you have been badly treated by the Inland Revenue, your case can be considered by an impartial referee known as the Revenue Adjudicator (see also p. 165). You must, however, give the tax office concerned the chance to settle your complaint before going to the Adjudicator (see leaflet *You and the Inland Revenue*).

- **NATIONAL INSURANCE** Most working people aged between 16 and state pensionable age must pay contributions into the National Insurance (NI) scheme in order to qualify for NI benefits, such as retirement pensions, unemployment benefit, incapacity benefit, maternity allowance and widow's benefit. The Contributions Agency is responsible for handling NI contributions, levels of which for employers, employees and the self-employed are set by the Government in the Budget.

Your NI number is your unique reference which records all the contributions you have paid during your working life. You should have received your number before your 16th birthday. If you have never had a number, or have lost it, get in touch with your Contributions Agency office. Your employer will need to know your NI number, or your Contributions

Agency office will need it if you are self-employed. Your Benefits Agency office will also ask you for it if you claim benefits.

- **CLASSES OF CONTRIBUTIONS** There are five classes of National Insurance contribution:

- Class 1 – paid by employees and their employers subject to earnings thresholds (see leaflet *NP 28 National Insurance for employees* or phone the Social Security Advice Line for Employers on 0800 393 539);

- Class 1A – paid by employers who provide their employees with car fuel and/or a car for private use (see leaflet *NI 280 Cars and fuel*);

- Class 2 – paid by the self-employed at a flat rate. Self-employed people may claim exemption from payment of Class 2 contributions if their profits are expected to be below a certain level for the tax year. They are not eligible for unemployment and industrial injuries benefits;

- Class 3 – paid voluntarily to safeguard rights to some benefits (see leaflet *NI 42 National Insurance voluntary contributions*); and

- Class 4 – paid by self-employed people (in addition to their Class 2 contributions) on their taxable profits over a set limit.

More information for the self-employed is available in the leaflets *IR 24 Class 4 National Insurance contributions* (available from the Inland Revenue), *NP 18 Class 2 and Class 4 National Insurance contributions for self-employed people,* and *NI 27A National Insurance for people with small earnings from self-employment.*

If you are liable for contributions and pay late, you may forfeit your rights to certain social security benefits or reduce the amount you would otherwise have received (see leaflet *NI 48 National Insurance – unpaid and late paid contributions*).

Employees who work after pensionable age do not pay contributions but the employer continues to be liable. Self-employed people over pensionable age do not pay contributions.

In some circumstances you may be eligible for NI credits, for instance for the tax years containing your 16th, 17th and 18th birthdays. Some married women and widows still have the right to pay reduced rate contributions.

● FURTHER INFORMATION

Details about current tax rules, rates, allowances and reliefs can be found in a range of explanatory leaflets available from your local tax office or tax enquiry centre (under Inland Revenue in the phone book). Which? magazine publishes annual guides on how to save tax. **The Revenue Adjudicator's Office** is located at 3rd floor, Haymarket House, 28 Haymarket, London SW1Y 4SP (Tel. 0171 930 2292). Leaflets on National Insurance are available from **Contributions Agency** offices (see under **Contributions Agency** or **Social Security** in the phone book).

Debt

Seeking help with debt • Going to court • Bankruptcy

It is usually possible to sort out a debt problem if action is taken promptly. Some debts need to be dealt with urgently. You may, for example, be faced with:

- disconnection of household services;

- court action for possession of your home;

- bankruptcy; or

- imprisonment for non-payment of a fine, maintenance, child support or council tax.

Often a person with one debt that has become urgent will have other debts. You should not try to deal with one debt in isolation. Debts should all be considered at the same time because it is important that creditors know your full financial situation.

- **WHAT CAN A CREDITOR DO?** A creditor who is pressing you for payment may not be aware of your financial circumstances. If the creditor is told about those circumstances and that you are getting money advice, he or she may agree to accept reduced payments or no payments at all. Creditors are allowed to send reminders to someone who is in debt, but they are not allowed to resort to improper methods. They are not allowed to telephone you during unsociable hours or repeatedly at work, nor can they contact your employer. Creditors cannot falsely threaten you with criminal proceedings. If you feel that the creditors are using improper methods you should contact your local trading standards department or the police.

• **WHERE SHOULD I SEEK ADVICE?** If you have debt problems you should first seek specialist advice. Before seeing an adviser, gather together all the papers which relate to your finances, including any court papers and letters, bills and credit agreements, and details of your income.

If you have to wait for an appointment, it may be helpful to tell your creditors that you have contacted an adviser for help. Most creditors welcome the involvement of a specialist adviser. They may be willing to delay action to enable an agreement to be reached.

Help and advice about debt problems are available from:

• Citizens Advice Bureaux (who may refer you, if it is a complicated case, to a money advice specialist, who may be a solicitor or insolvency practitioner);

• money advice centres and law centres (see also p. 129);

• the Money Advice Association (Tel. 0171 236 3566); and

• the National Debt Line (which gives free information to people living in England and Wales and provides an information pack dealing with debt – Tel. 0121 359 8501).

The addresses and phone numbers of local Citizens Advice Bureaux, money advice centres and law centres can be found in the telephone directory.

• **WHAT IF ADVICE IS NOT AVAILABLE?** If you are trying to resolve a debt problem yourself, you should take the following steps:

• work out your disposable income and your outgoings to see how much is left to pay off the debts;

• deal with priority debts first (those which, if unpaid, have serious repercussions – see p. 157);

• get in touch with your creditors to see if they would be prepared to accept smaller payments over a longer period; and

• check whether you are claiming all the benefits and tax relief that you may be entitled to.

It is usually best not to borrow more money to pay off debts.

- **WHAT HAPPENS IF MY CREDITORS TAKE COURT ACTION AGAINST ME?** Creditors generally use court action as a last resort to recover debts. You should contact the local law centre or Citizens Advice Bureau to get free advice on how you should proceed. You will receive a court summons (usually from the county court) setting out the case against you and forms that you must fill in and return as soon as possible.

If you dispute the debt you should fill in the defence section of the reply form, setting out your case clearly. If you agree that you owe the money, you should fill in the admission section of the reply form. Even if you do not dispute the debt, you can still ask for time to pay. You must attend any court hearings that are arranged. If you are asking for more time to pay, take written evidence of your financial situation with you.

- **WHAT WILL HAPPEN AFTER THE COURT HEARING?** You will be sent the judgment of the court after the hearing. If you have been instructed to make payments, you will be sent details of the instalments you should make. The money is paid directly to the creditor by a method agreed between you. If there is any change in your future circumstances you can apply to the court for the instalments to be varied. Your name, address and details of the debt will be entered on the public register of county court judgments (unless the action was in the High Court). Having your debt recorded in this way will usually affect your chances of getting credit in the future. If you pay off the debt within one month you should ask the court to cancel the entry.

- **WHAT IF I FAIL TO PAY THE INSTALMENTS?** A creditor can ask the court for further action to be taken to recover a debt if you fail to pay the instalments. Through an attachment of earnings order, a deduction can be made from your wages or salary and paid to the creditor until the debt is cleared. A creditor can ask the court for an order to seize any money you have in a bank or other account, or for a charging order to be made, which means that you cannot sell your home without first paying your creditors. A creditor can also ask for the bailiff to seize and sell goods owned by you to pay off the debt.

- **CAN I BE MADE BANKRUPT?** Bankruptcy can have serious repercussions and it is important to seek specialist advice if faced with the prospect.

A creditor who is owed £750 can start the legal process to make you bankrupt. If, following a court judgment against you for a valid debt, the money ordered by the court to be paid to the creditor is not paid, then the creditor can use that 'judgment debt' to justify bringing a Creditor's Petition for bankruptcy. Alternatively, if the debt is above a certain amount and is not disputed, the creditor can serve a formal demand for payment on you. This demand is called a Statutory Demand, giving you 21 days to repay the debt. Failure to repay will result in the creditor presenting a Creditor's Petition, which will start the bankruptcy process.

- **CAN I MAKE MYSELF BANKRUPT?** You can file a petition for your own bankruptcy; this is known as a Debtor's Petition (an expensive procedure). You will also have to complete a Statement of Affairs giving full details of your assets and liabilities. The court will then make a bankruptcy order. In certain instances the court may appoint an insolvency practitioner to see if voluntary arrangements with creditors can be made and bankruptcy avoided.

- **IF I AM MADE BANKRUPT WILL EVERYTHING BE TAKEN FROM ME?** If you are made bankrupt your assets and possessions can be seized, apart from basic items such as clothing and household equipment. Possessions owned solely by your partner or spouse cannot be seized. If you own the family home and have a wife and child living there, the court may order the postponement of the sale for up to 12 months. The trustee in bankruptcy can ask the court to make an Income Payments Order, which requires the employer to pay some of your wages directly towards your debt.

- **HOW LONG DOES THE BANKRUPTCY LAST?** Normally a bankrupt is automatically discharged from bankruptcy after three years (after two years in certain circumstances). If someone has been made bankrupt twice within a fifteen-year period, the bankruptcy will not be discharged for five years and an application must be made to the court. The discharged bankrupt cannot reclaim property from the trustee in bankruptcy. Some debts will remain after discharge; for instance, the trustee may sell assets such as the family home at any time in the future.

Political rights, complaints systems • and legal redress

Political rights, complaints systems and legal redress

- **THE RIGHT TO VOTE** You have the right to vote in elections to the House of Commons, the European Parliament and local government authorities if you are:
- 18 years of age or over;
- a British citizen or citizen of another Commonwealth country or the Irish Republic; and
- on the electoral register. (To be entered on the annual register, which comes into force on 16 February, you must be resident in the constituency on the previous 10 October.)

If you are a citizen of another member state of the European Union, you can vote in elections to the European Parliament but not in elections to the House of Commons. The right to vote at local government elections will be extended to citizens of other member states in 1996.

The electoral register is compiled each year by electoral registration officers. It is a criminal offence to refuse to give to the officer the information he or she needs for the register, or to give false information.

- **STANDING FOR OFFICE**

House of Commons elections

If you wish to stand for election to the House of Commons, you must be nominated by at least ten people registered to vote in the constituency. You also have to pay a deposit of £500, which is returned to you if you get more than 5 per cent of the votes cast. You cannot become a Member of Parliament if you:

- are not a British citizen, a citizen of another Commonwealth country or an Irish citizen;
- are under the age of 21 years;
- are seriously mentally ill;
- are a member of the clergy, including a minister of the Churches of England, Scotland or Ireland, or a Roman Catholic priest;
- are a peer in the House of Lords;
- have been bankrupt or have been discharged from bankruptcy in the last five years;
- hold certain jobs – for example, if you are a member of the armed forces, judge or a full-time police officer;
- are serving a prison sentence of more than one year; or
- have been convicted of certain electoral offences and have been disqualified from being an MP.

European elections

In the case of elections to the European Parliament, peers, members of the clergy and existing members of the British Parliament can stand as candidates, as can nationals of other member states of the European Union. Candidates must be nominated by 30 electors in the constituency and a deposit of £1,000 must be paid; this is returned if the candidate gets more than 5 per cent of votes cast.

Local elections

If you wish to be a local councillor, you must be over 21 years of age and be a British or other Commonwealth citizen or an Irish citizen. You must also:

- be resident in the area of the local authority concerned in the 12 months before nomination as a candidate; or
- be a local government elector for the area; or
- own or rent property in the area; or
- have your main place of work in the area in the 12 months before nomination as a candidate.

You are not eligible to be elected to sit as a councillor for the local authority if you are an employee of that authority. You can be an employee of another authority unless you hold a senior restricted post or carry out certain politically sensitive activities such as public relations work or advising committees or local politicians.

If you wish to be a candidate, you must be nominated by ten electors in the ward you are standing for. You do not need to pay a deposit.

- **COMPLAINTS SYSTEM** If you want to complain about the service provided by government departments and public bodies, your first port of call is the internal complaints procedure of the body concerned. If these procedures are exhausted and you are dissatisfied with the way in which your complaint has been handled, you can have your grievance considered by the various Ombudsman schemes.

- **CENTRAL GOVERNMENT** If you have a complaint to make about maladministration by a government department or agency, send the details to any MP at the House of Commons, London SW1A 0AA, or to his or her local constituency office. Alternatively the complaint may be made to any MP on your behalf by a Citizens Advice Bureau or a professional adviser such as a lawyer.

If the MP considers your complaint justified, he or she can make a direct approach to the department or public authority concerned to put the grievance right, or send details to the Ombudsman – officially called the Parliamentary Commissioner for Administration – whose jurisdiction covers central government departments and a large number of non-departmental public bodies.

The Ombudsman's jurisdiction is confined to maladministration such as serious delay in dealing with correspondence, discourtesy, failure to follow proper procedures and mistakes in the handling of social security claims or tax matters. If the Ombudsman thinks that your case involves maladministration and upholds your complaint, the department or public body is expected to put things right. Remedies include the giving of an apology, financial compensation or changes in administration to prevent things going wrong again.

- **LOCAL GOVERNMENT** Complaints about maladministration by local government authorities are considered by independent Commissioners for Local Administration, often known as Local Government Ombudsmen. There are three of these in England and one in Wales. You must first give the local authority the chance to deal with the problem under its own complaints procedure. If you are dissatisfied with the outcome, you can ask your local councillor to look into the matter. If the issue is not resolved, you can send a complaint to your Ombudsman or ask your councillor to do this for you.

If the Ombudsman considers that maladministration has occurred, the local council must consider the report and inform the ombudsman of the action it proposes to take. Councils can pay compensation to you or take other action to put things right.

- **THE NATIONAL HEALTH SERVICE** If you wish to complain about National Health Service authorities, you can have your complaint considered by the Health Service Commissioners (one each for England and Wales – see also p. 88). You must, however, complain first to the health service authority so that it can mount an investigation. The Health Service Commissioner's jurisdiction does not extend to complaints about clinical judgments or family practitioners.

- **INLAND REVENUE** If you feel that you have been badly treated by your taxation office, your case can be considered by an impartial referee known as the Revenue Adjudicator. You must, however, give the Inland Revenue the chance to settle your complaint before going to the Adjudicator, who rules on complaints about excessive delay, discourtesy and the way the tax authorities exercise their discretion. The Adjudicator tries to help the two parties come to an agreement but if this fails, a formal recommendation can be made to the tax authorities on ways of settling the complaint. You are entitled to ask your MP to pass a complaint about the tax authorities to the Parliamentary Ombudsman even if your complaint has first been looked at by the Revenue Adjudicator.

- **PENSIONS** You are entitled by law to complain to the Pensions Ombudsman, who considers disputes about occupational and personal pensions schemes (see also p. 117). You are expected to try to sort out the matter first with the trustees, manager or employer. If not satisfied, you should go to the Occupational Pensions Advisory Service, which is an independent organisation with local expert pensions advisers. If the Service fails to solve the problem, you can send your complaint to the Pensions Ombudsman, who decides whether action by the pensions scheme or the employer is needed. The decision is binding on both sides and can be appealed only on a point of law to the High Court.

- **HOUSING ASSOCIATION OMBUDSMAN** Housing associations are the main providers of additional low-cost housing for rent and sale to people on low incomes and in the greatest housing need. If you have a complaint about maladministration, you should send it to your association. If the complaint is not resolved, you have the right to ask the Housing Association Ombudsman to investigate. If the Ombudsman finds in your favour, he or she may recommend a payment to cover your costs.

- **LEGAL SERVICES OMBUDSMEN** If you have a complaint to make about a solicitor, barrister or licensed conveyancer, you have the right to complain to the appropriate professional body. If you are dissatisfied with the way the body handles your complaint, you can ask the Legal Services Ombudsman in England and Wales to investigate. The Ombudsman has power to criticise the professional body and to recommend the payment of compensation for loss or inconvenience.

- **COMPLAINTS AGAINST THE POLICE** Complaints against the police in England and Wales may be supervised by the Police Complaints Authority (PCA). If you wish to make a complaint, you should go to your local police authority. An investigating officer is appointed by the deputy chief constable and a supervisor by the PCA. The investigating officer writes a summary report, which is submitted to the PCA, together with a copy of the evidence, transcripts and statements. A copy of the report is sent to the Crown Prosecution Service if there is evidence that police officers have broken the law. A similar investigation takes place in the case of complaints not supervised by the PCA. Under the complaints system, a police officer can be disciplined if there is evidence that police disciplinary codes have been broken.

- **THE COURTS** You are entitled to claim your rights in the law courts, which can and do intervene if you seek a legal remedy for an injury arising from the act or omission of a public authority. In addition, the courts have wider powers to review action taken by government ministers and officials. These judicial reviews make sure that proper authority is given to a public body by Parliament and that these powers are not exceeded. Applications for judicial review by individuals or groups are decided by a High Court judge. If granted, the review is conducted by three High Court judges who have the power to criticise a minister's action and quash his or her decision. They can also prevent a public authority from acting contrary to the rules of natural justice.

- **TRIBUNALS** You can also obtain redress from administrative tribunals, which deal with more than one million cases a year. They are independent of government and adjudicate on your rights on issues such as social security, taxation and employment. Tribunals normally consist of three people, who hear the case and decide the issue on the basis of the evidence submitted by both parties. There is a right of appeal on a point of law from many tribunals to the High Court in England and Wales. Leaflets explaining tribunal procedures and the remedies available can be found at your local social security or tax office or the Council on Tribunals.

Transport: rights and obligations •

Overseas travel •

Transport: rights and obligations

Private motoring • Taxis • Motor cycles • Bicycles • Bus/coach travel •
Train travel • Travelling by sea • Air travel • Further information

What are my formal obligations as a private motorist?
You must have a valid driving licence and your vehicle should be road-worthy, properly registered, taxed and insured.

How do I get a driving licence?
By passing a driving test. To learn to drive, you must get a provisional driving licence, for which you must be at least 17 years of age and medically fit to drive (application forms from your local post office). It is best to take driving lessons from an Approved Driving Instructor, registered with the Driving Standards Agency.

Driving licences are usually valid until the age of 70, after which they must be sent for renewal every three years. Renewal is automatic, unless there has been a change in the holder's medical circumstances, when another driving test may be necessary. There is currently no upper age limit on driving a car. Proposals are in hand to introduce photographs on driving licences after 1996.

What about registration, tax and insurance?
A car must be registered in the name of the person who keeps it on the road. A new car is usually registered for you by the dealer; if you buy a second-hand car, you must get the registration document from the seller, complete and send it to the Driver and Vehicle Licensing Agency (DVLA). (These procedures are under review and may be subject to change.) Car tax must be paid every year, and the tax disc correctly displayed on the windscreen of your vehicle. If your vehicle is over three years old, it must

have a valid vehicle test (MOT) certificate; the test must be carried out by a testing centre appointed by the Vehicle Inspectorate.

You must have valid third-party insurance covering your use of the vehicle.

What are my obligations on the road?

You must observe the speed limits, traffic signals and road markings and any directions given by the police. You must drive safely, with consideration for other road users. You should observe the Highway Code.

What are my obligations towards my passengers?

You are responsible for ensuring that children (under 14 years) in the front seat are restrained and in the rear seat where child restraints and seat belts are fitted. Passengers aged 14 and over are individually responsible for making sure they are wearing seat belts and must do so in cars where belts are fitted.

Are there any circumstances in which I should NOT drive?

You must not drive under the influence of drugs or drink. If you develop a medical condition which may affect your driving, you must report this to the Driver and Vehicle Licensing Agency.

What about taking a taxi?

There are about 50,000 licensed taxis in England and Wales. In London and several other major cities taxis must be purpose-built to conform to strict requirements and new ones have to provide for people in wheelchairs. In smaller towns and rural areas taxis are usually saloon cars. Licensed taxis may be hired in the street or at a taxi rank. Fares in London are set by the Government, and by local authorities in the rest of England and Wales. Taximeters must be clearly visible to the passenger and the driver must not charge more than the amount shown. You are not legally obliged to offer a tip. If you have a complaint about a licensed London taxi you should contact the Public Carriage Office (Tel. 0171 230 1631), or the local authority outside London.

Private hire vehicles with drivers (minicabs) must not be hired on the street but must be booked in advance through the operator.

What about riding a motor cycle/moped?

You must have a provisional licence to ride as a learner and take a basic training course with an approved training body *before* you ride on the road. You must pass a motor cycle driving test within two years or your provisional licence will be withdrawn for a year. All motor cyclists and passengers must wear safety helmets. Pillion passengers must sit on a proper seat behind the driver and be able to reach the footrests. You should follow the Highway Code.

And riding a bicycle?

You should obey the Highway Code's provisions for cyclists. It is wise to wear a cycle helmet, and light-coloured or fluorescent clothing.

What are my obligations when travelling by bus/coach?

You must buy a ticket appropriate to your journey, in accordance with the operator's conditions of issue. Your rights and responsibilities are defined by the operator's conditions of carriage. However, for these to be legally binding the operator must have taken reasonable steps to inform you of them.

Your conduct on any public service vehicle is governed by regulations which prohibit behaviour that causes annoyance, offence or danger to anyone else on the vehicle. If you contravene these regulations, the driver, conductor or inspector may have you removed.

What are the bus company's responsibilities to its passengers?

Local bus services must be registered with the Traffic Commissioner and must be run on the route and to the timetable registered. If the company wants to introduce a new service, change or cancel an existing service, it must give the Traffic Commissioner six weeks' notice. Express coach services (those with stopping places more than 15 miles apart) do not have to be registered.

The conduct of bus crews is governed by regulations and the company is responsible for keeping its vehicles properly maintained and for ensuring the safety of passengers at all times when on the vehicle, and when boarding or alighting.

What if I have a complaint?

First contact the bus company. All operators have conditions of carriage, which should be available on request. Many bus and coach companies have also joined the Confederation of Passenger Transport's Quality Code and Code of Practice on Customer Complaints. These bind the company to responding to complaints within one week in most circumstances.

If you wish to complain about a general lack of bus services, contact your local authority to see if they would be prepared to subsidise more services. If you suspect that a company's vehicles are not well maintained in any way or that your local bus service is not running on time, contact the Traffic Commissioner for your region.

What are my rights and responsibilities when travelling by train?

Your legal rights and responsibilities are set out in British Rail's published Conditions of Carriage, which cover passengers and luggage and set the limits for compensation; copies are available from major stations.

What are British Rail's commitments to its customers?

British Rail's Passenger's Charter states its commitment to meeting performance standards of punctuality and reliability; providing accurate, timely and up-to-date details of fares, services and facilities; and making travel easier for disabled passengers. It explains what will be done to keep travellers informed and to look after them if things go wrong, and how to claim compensation for delays or cancellations. Copies are available from major stations.

What if I have a complaint?

You should contact the train operator concerned (addresses are shown on posters at your local station or in your phone book). You can also write to one of the independent Rail Users' Consultative Committees (addresses from stations or from rail timetables).

What are my rights and responsibilities when travelling by ferry?

Passengers, their luggage and vehicles are subject to the Conditions of Carriage of the operating company. These are available from the company's offices and contain information about the carrier's liability for injury, loss or damage and for delay or deviation.

What about safety on roll-on/roll-off ferries?

Shipowners have a duty to ensure the safe operation of their vessels and have to comply with a wide range of technical measures.

What are an airline's responsibilities towards its passengers?
Airlines and passengers are bound by the Conditions of Contract printed at the back of the ticket. Topics include baggage, timetables and stopping places. Passengers are required to comply with the Government's travel requirements, have the necessary travel documents and arrive at the airport in time.

Are there restrictions on what I can carry in my baggage?
These are printed at the front of your airline ticket: they include corrosive, explosive and poisonous substances and other dangerous articles.

What if my flight is delayed or cancelled?
A ticket only obliges the airline to take you between two airports; there is no obligation to do so at the time printed on your ticket. If a flight is delayed or cancelled because of bad weather or mechanical trouble on the aircraft, many airlines provide food and drink while you wait, though they are not obliged to do so.

What if my flight is overbooked?
If this happens to you at an airport in the European Union, Norway, Iceland, or the USA, and there are no seats left on the plane, you are entitled to immediate cash compensation provided your booking has been confirmed and you have arrived at the check-in desk in time.

What if I have a complaint?
You should contact the Customer Relations Department of the airline or the Customer Services Department of the airport. You can also write to the Air Transport Users' Council.

FURTHER INFORMATION

The address of the **Air Transport Users' Council** is: 5th floor, Kingsway House, 103 Kingsway, London WC2B 6QX. You can contact the **Driver and Vehicle Licensing Agency** by writing to DVLA, Swansea SA99 1AB.

Overseas travel

Passports • Visas • Other requirements • Medical treatment • Duty-free •
Problems abroad • Safety • Further information

What kind of passport do I need?

Everyone travelling overseas needs to carry a valid passport, although children under the age of 16 can be included on their parents' passports.

A standard ten-year British passport is valid for all countries, although in some cases you may also need a visa from the country concerned (see p. 176). An application form for a passport can be obtained from a main post office, a Passport Office, or some travel agents; it includes all the necessary information on how to complete the form and apply for the passport. Send or take your application form and the fee to a Passport Office (listed on the form) at least a month before you need the passport. Between February and June, when most people apply for passports, your application may take longer to process. If you need a passport sooner, you can phone a Passport Office for advice.

The Government approved the UK Passport Agency's recommendation that the one-year British Visitors Passport be withdrawn from 1 January 1996.

Another travel document – the British Excursion Document for short-stay travel to France – was withdrawn from 1 March 1995.

When do I need a visa?

Some countries require you to have a visa in addition to your passport. In some cases visas can be obtained at the border when you enter the country concerned, but in the case of other countries you have to apply well in advance, normally at the embassy or consulate of the country concerned. The UK Passport Agency publishes a booklet which gives details of current requirements and also gives the addresses and telephone numbers of the consulates of the foreign embassies in London.

If you are in any doubt about visas, it is worth checking, as visa requirements change from time to time. It is also worth bearing in mind that foreign consulates are often only open for a limited period each day and that they may make a charge for the visa. They may also request additional information and may take some time to process visa applications.

Are there any other official requirements before I travel?

Some countries require you to have inoculations against particular diseases; in other cases inoculations or other medical precautions – such as taking anti-malaria tablets – are not compulsory but are advised by medical experts. Details can be obtained from your doctor or from the London School of Hygiene and Tropical Medicine (Keppel Street, London WC1E 7HT – Tel. 0171 636 8636). Guide books provide another useful source of information about medical requirements for particular countries. You should seek any medical advice well in advance.

What if I need medical treatment abroad?

National Health Service medical treatment is not available if you are travelling outside Britain. It is your responsibility to make alternative arrangements, normally through one of the numerous private travel insurance schemes. However, if you are travelling in European Union countries you are entitled to treatment on the same terms as the countries' own citizens. In order to receive such treatment you will need *Form E111*. You will find the application form in a booklet available from post offices. The form should be obtained before you travel.

In some other countries there are separate agreements which entitle British citizens to medical treatment on the same terms as local citizens. You can find out about these from the Department of Health International Relations Unit, Room 310, Hannibal House, Elephant and Castle, London SE1 6TE.

You should bear in mind that the treatment on offer in other countries may not be on the same terms as NHS treatment and you may need to pay.

What can I bring back from abroad?

On re-entering Britain you must pass through HM Customs at the port or airport. You must not carry any illegal substance, such as dangerous drugs. There are restrictions on, for example, the import of animals and plants. There are also limits on the amounts of other items, such as alcoholic drinks and cigarettes and other tobacco products, which you can bring into Britain without paying duty or tax on each item. Details of these limits are available from your local enquiry office of HM Customs and Excise (see under Customs and Excise in the phone book).

There is no legal limit on the amount of any product which people can bring in to the country from other European Union countries, but such goods must be only for the traveller's personal use. HM Customs and Excise has set advisory limits for the amount people can bring into the country. You can find this out from your local enquiry office.

What if I experience problems abroad?

British embassies and consulates can provide help to you abroad in the event of serious problems. Consuls can offer advice, and assist in cases involving transfer of funds, deaths, hospitalisation and arrests. Embassies and consulates cannot help with travel arrangements, accommodation or work permits.

You can find the addresses and telephone numbers of British embassies and consulates in *HM Diplomatic Service Overseas Reference List*, produced by the Foreign & Commonwealth Office.

Is it safe to travel to a particular country?

If you are concerned that it may be unsafe to travel to a particular country or part of the world, you can get up-to-date advice from the Foreign & Commonwealth Office Travel Advice Unit (Tel. 0171 270 4129/79). Always bear in mind that situations in some countries can change rapidly.

● FURTHER INFORMATION

The application for Form E111 is to be found at the back of a booklet entitled Health Advice for Travellers. Advice about travel in the European Union can also be obtained from the UK Office of the **Commission of the European Communities** (Jean Monnet House, 8 Storey's Gate, London SW1P 3AT – Tel. 0171 973 1992). The **UK Passport Agency** can be contacted on 0171 279 3434.

Index

Printed in the United Kingdom for HMSO.
Dd.0301542, 12/95, C50, 3400, 5673, 335105.